ALONG THE RIVER

A NOTE ON THE AUTHOR

Richard Fountaine was born and brought up in Surrey, England, in a family that had farming, legal, and mountaineering backgrounds. He went to Trinity College Dublin, and Exeter College Oxford, and variously studied English literature, history, economics, politics, geology, history of music and education. He then took up law, working in London. His philosophical, anti-whaling novel, *Tisala*, was published in 2015 under the pen name Richard Seward Newton. He has been a lifelong writer of poems. In recent years he has returned to Oxford to research the history of poetry.

ALONG THE RIVER

Poems 1960-2020

Richard Fountaine

Ⓜ
BLUE MARK BOOKS

First published in Great Britain by
Blue Mark Books Limited in 2022

www.bluemarkbooks.com

© Richard Fountaine, 2022

The moral rights of the author have been asserted

A catalogue record for this book is
available from the British Library

ISBN 978-1-910369-22-7

All rights reserved. No part of this publication may be reproduced, stored
in any retrieval system or electronic system, or transmitted, in any form or
by any means without the prior written permission of the publisher, nor
be lent, resold, hired out or otherwise circulated in any form of binding or
cover other than that in which is it published and without a similar
condition being imposed on the subsequent purchaser

Blue Mark Books Limited supports the Forest Stewardship Council®. The
FSC® promotes the responsible management of the world's forests.
All our books carrying the FSC® logo are printed on FSC®-certified paper

Typeset in Adobe Caslon Pro by
Blue Mark Books Limited

Printed and bound in Great Britain by
TJ Books Limited, Padstow.

To my family

and

*for all those who can find something of
value or enjoyment along this river*

Contents

Introduction	1
Preface	3

The Opening Stream

The Target	27
This Unassuming Beauty	29
What Shall I Feel?	30
The Student's Dilemma	31
Salute to the Cinema	32
Town Bands in Germany	33
Weather and Authority	34
Springtime in a Coppice	36
The Cuban Crisis	37
A Student's Turmoil	38
Forebears and Descendants	40
We Were Gods	41
A Seabird's Life and Death	42
I Felt the Challenge	43
After Glandular Fever	44
How Can I Work?	45
Hope and Sadness	46
Topography of Love	47
I Sent My Love	48
What Shall I Say?	49
I Shall Not Praise This Greece	50
Shakespeare's England	51

The Broader River

In Persia, 1974	55
Thank You Letter to the Poets	58
The Trails of Poetry	59
In The City, Seminars	63
All Those Grey Solicitors	65
Fortieth Birthday	66
New Year's Eve Party	67
The Princess	68
Since By My Age	69
Two Universes	70
Four Fires	71
Time	73
Sleep	74
Heavenly Physics	75
On the Nature of Luck	76
Victoria's Vespers	77
From Tisala	78
The Story of the Stars and Gods	79
The Butterfly and the Spider	83
On Hearing the News from Yugoslavia	85
China Recalled	86
In a Chinese Home	88
Children of India	89
Children of India II	90
The Two Gifts	91
On The Unexpected Death of a Japanese Friend	92
At the Ballet	93
The Master Class	94

The Quiet Flow

Tess	99
Age	101
I Hope When I am Dead	102
The Golden Coin	103
Windle	104
Miss Adams	105
The Photographs Not Taken	106
Autumn Leaves	107
When My Body Dies	108
Life and Giving Way	110

More Fun on the Riverbank

The Seasons' Compromise	113
Freddie	114
Travel, Gin and Wine in India	115
On Reading too Many Poems for a Poetry Competition	117
The Ballad of Tom Drinker	118
Pop Lyric	119
The Ballad of Felix Cavalier	120
Notes	123
Acknowledgements	139

Introduction

Like many people with some awareness of literary history, I want poetry to have a more important place in the modern world than it often has, certainly in the West. In previous times, among the educated in most civilisations, it was deemed to be of central importance to culture and civilised society. Poetry was to reflect its age, but also to help shape it, both in the public and private spheres of life.

The Preface to these poems puts forward this view as expressed by poets and writers in the past. In doing so it criticises the trend of much twentieth-century poetry for its perceived departure from this aspiration, and its failure to engage sufficiently with much of importance in our world.

A more universal aim and role for poetry is arguably needed more than ever in our complicated world where the sheer scale and power of political forces, industry and technology can also tend to dehumanise lives and society.

Readers of the Preface will see that I have argued for particular qualities in poetry – a wide engagement with the world, clarity, comprehensibility and enjoyment. In the light of such an approach I should give a short background note on my own poems. Whether they will be found successful in these respects will be decided by readers. Some may prefer to read the poems first, and come to the viewpoint argued in the Preface afterwards.

These poems have been written across nearly sixty years. A few from my youth are included. Some of these lean on the style of earlier poets. Certainly my generation was educated and immersed in the long tradition of English poetry. But if my poems are thereby a link to the past, I hope that as time went on they have become, though without any conscious plan, a bridge to the present; and perhaps even a little into the future, both in the range of subject matter and form.

With regard to form, I found that in valuing clarity and understanding, I tended to favour a familiar basis, such as the iambic pentameter, but re-worked more freely through experiencing free verse forms, while retaining a recognisable rhythm and structure. Some have questioned whether or not the traditional full-rhyme lyric or sonnet can still validly be written. From my earlier poems, a few of this type are included for readers' consideration.

On the order of the poems and their subject matter, I have tried to make a sort of narrative by linkage between the poems. For instance, it seemed sensible to put the loves and troubles of youth in the first part of the book. But politics and world events enter into it, and poems exploring views of life. So the picture widens out – history, religion, the sciences and so on, but also interweaving the personal in a journey through life. And in the end, fun outplaces age, as it should, so long as possible. The Notes give some context and background information.

Richard Fountaine, September 2022

Preface
The aim and role of poetry in the past and present

Is poetry in trouble, and if so does it much matter when the whole world, despite our many advances, also seems also to be in an increasingly tumultuous and disordered state? A world of overpopulation, with struggles for economic and national superiority feeding into climatic dangers for the whole planet; with violence and wars, and millions of displaced refugees; and on-going battles against the spreading of disease. To which the poet answers, yes, because poetry can, in its own way sometimes uniquely, illuminate and enhance life for the individual, and serve as a lighthouse to civilisation.

The indispensable function of poetry is to draw us rewardingly into a world created by words and imagination, aiming to illuminate the world in its many aspects. No other art is succinct enough while also being cumulatively comprehensive in its range. A film or painting may marvellously tell a story, but is fixed. Poetry, like music, can be reinterpreted. But while music and poetry both have strong emotional powers in matters of the human spirit, music lacks the rational faculty and image-creating scope of words. It is not in music's essential function to explore science, the clash of religions and beliefs, economics, climate change or the environmental future. Novels are too long to be retained in the same way as poetry. Poetry can provide memorable insights by combining ideas in words and phrases, quotations and echoes that can enhance and become integrally part of our lives and culture. The lighthouse can be beautiful as well as important.

My broad thesis is this: there is a desire for the poetic in human life, for beauty, empathy, love, unsatisfied both by much modern poetry and the way the world is developing. To understand the modern world the sheer amount of knowledge and information (scientific, historical and social) required is vast. No-one and no one group commands it. Certainly, twentieth-century poets did not. They never mastered the scope of the industrial, scientific and technological upheavals taking place; nor their worldwide impact on people and societies through politics, demographics and religious culture.

Yet poetry is a form of language which, in its small compass, can be readily recollected. It could and should be a perfect vehicle for ordering, reflecting and illuminating the modern world. Recognised twentieth-century poetry has in this largely fallen short, or at least it has not risen to that particular challenge. The net result is the diminution of the role of the poetry in society. In this wider world, poetry is regarded as of marginal relevance at best. Of course, there are many external reasons for this – radio, television, digital media, the tenor of the times – but poetry itself bears some responsibility. Often, the individual interests of the poet's imagination are given precedence over readers' enjoyment. The reader has to try to follow the poets into their own, often difficult or fragmented-imaged world, rather than the poets illuminating what for most readers is the real recognisable world of their experience, both personal and in the wider sphere.

If this is true, it may lead us to look at the poets perhaps differently, to see where greatness, weakness and limitations lay and lie, always with the view of encouraging a new sort of writing that may help promote the valuable place of poetry in the cultures of civilised society. For that to happen, poetry has to become popular with a wide range of the public. It must inspire an imaginative, emotional, intellectual experience and excitement that is often lacking in too much 'difficult' modern poetry. At one level it is now largely the preserve of movements or groupings of people united in setting or following favoured poetic trends. (There is an older generation, who were brought up and educated with a wide range of earlier poetry, but they are now passing). At another level there is the pop, rag, folk and performance poetry popular amongst the young; but which mainly relies on fragmentary words and emotions, often backed by a particular and limited music. These contribute, but neither fulfils the hunger for a more universal, ordered poetic human voice, and the delight of understanding life in what is an increasingly complicated, urban and industrial world.

In making these criticisms there is a danger of appearing negative. There is no doubt at all that much good poetry is being written. One of the difficulties in our rapidly changing world is getting it into the mainstream consciousness. This has many aspects. Academic convention tends to follow retrospectively movements in poetry, and look for the next experiment in cultural development. Traditional publishing tries to follow suit, but has issues of commercial viability. Enterprising efforts have been made to boost poetry, by dedicated small presses, broadcasting, such as 'Poetry Please', and initiatives such as 'Poems on the Underground'. But perhaps the criticism is needed to encourage the flowering of a new age of poetry.

Looked at in this light, various thoughts and themes on twentieth and early twenty-first-century poetry began to form, first into a hunch and then hypothesis, as to what was happening to our poetic wellsprings; and from that, perhaps what is needed. And I found there were like minds among some critics and commentators, some of who are quoted or referred to below.

But first there is a deck-clearing question to ask: has the form of poetry used in the twentieth century contributed to its problems? There are a few things – apart from bad verse itself (tired images, forced rhyme, verb-less lists of words etc) – that can mar or destroy a poem. Free form can, of course, produce wonderful poetry, but can seem to be perversely random. A rhyming format can result in dated, trite or laboured verse, which may be why the Greeks did not use rhyme in their poetry. But rhyme well used often establishes the memorability of a poem, and this can be an important ingredient in its social and cultural usefulness.

Then there is punctuation. Its purpose is to help readers to read and understand. Sometimes, writers dispense with it entirely, perhaps to appear free or modern. It can achieve such a feel, but it puts most poems and their readers under a handicap from which they struggle to emerge. Authors sometimes appear to think that punctuation gets in the way of the poem's layers of meaning, but that never got in Shakespeare's way, or any other great poet's work.

And layers of meaning lead straight to the issue of incomprehensibility. Too often authors fail to establish the thought of the poem. Not infrequently the whole endeavour remains baffling because, although the writer knows what is intended, it has not been expressed or realised on the page. The writer may be trying to find some new angle, a new way of presenting thought and feeling and therefore wishes to avoid the obvious; but the danger is impenetrable obscurity. It is probably the most important reason why so much modern poetry fails to engage, let alone inspire a wider audience. The reader has better things to do than struggle with it unavailingly.

Many writers turn to poetry to express personal emotion – one of poetry's strongest motivations – but not always a sufficient one to ensure a good poem. Grief, loss and death, unsurprisingly given their importance in life, can be the stuff of powerful poems, (often to work out the poet's demons, like the unhappy Sylvia Plath); but despite the deep and genuine feelings of the writers, the desire to express these emotions is often not enough to engender a successful poem. Much of the difference lies in the competence of form already mentioned, and in the positive qualities discussed below. The danger of strong emotion for poetry-writers is that they feel so much when they write their lines that they think the reader must feel the same. This is not true. It depends largely on their words and the form of their words. Certainly, what the reader feels also partly depends on the reader's own makeup. The poet can do nothing about that. But usually people who read poetry are ready to respond to a poet's offering – that is why they read – and when they are disappointed the reason most times lies with the writer.

As argued above, poetry is a craft, and not one easily mastered. In the best poets, craft and the form of it has become second nature. But good poetry needs more than craft.

So, to ask 'How do you define good poetry?' may help in the writing of it. There are many definitions, including Coleridge's true but insufficiently helpful 'the right words in the right order'. The primary colours may perhaps be taken as something like this: poetry uses words memorably to illuminate from the particular true aspects of humanity and the world. If a poem is to illuminate it must first, and crucially, be comprehensible. But to illuminate also means to see in a new light. It entails linking up ideas so that reality is newly seen. It is not enough to be merely descriptive, even if well done. Two separate ideas linked with clarity produce nuggets of poetry: 'If music be the food of love play on'. Love and food are not immediate neighbours, but music feeding the emotions is immediately recognised as true. Shakespeare, as usual, does it effortlessly: 'The dawn in russet mantle clad.' And Dylan Thomas: 'The heron priested shore'. Images immediately recognised and understood as having truth. Memorability, even quotability, are key features of a good poetic culture, and are not normally available to long prose writing, such as novels.

Yet nuggets themselves are not enough. There are plenty of poems with telling phrases or lines where the poem itself is unsuccessful, often because of too many of the negatives mentioned above. A key element that turns writing into poetry is poetic rhythm. This is a definitive distinction between poetry and prose. In a good poem the rhythm is sustained throughout. It may change, like the rhythm and movements in a symphony, but it does not falter or clash and is seen and felt as integral to the whole, as in Coleridge's 'Kubla Khan'. And rhythm is more easily sustained if the poem has a discernible structure.

So much for the mechanics of poetry. There are two further aspects of poetry to address. The first is the purpose of it. And secondly how the twentieth-century poets rose, or did not rise, to that purpose. This leads to the criticism of the twentieth-century poets that follows below. By and large they reflected the perceived chaos of our times but were overwhelmed by it, and in that experience lost the wider function of poetry. They reflected and reacted to the age, but they did not change it, or make it. That required a more fundamental and rigorous engagement of knowledge and empathy with humanity and the wider world.

So, first a brief look at what earlier writers have thought was the purpose and calling of their art. This short essay cannot be a critical history, but merely a highlighting of ideas and pointers.

The Greeks and Romans tended to think of it in elevated terms. Aristotle, largely considering the poetry in Greek drama, thought the poets' role was to *use* tragedy and suffering to cleanse and renew humanity – catharsis - a form of spiritual release and uplift. Among Roman poets, Horace, the foremost lyric poet of his times, emphasised the poets' purpose to promote aesthetic values and social virtues by literary example, and thereby influenced poets as diverse as Ben Jonson, Pope, Byron and Auden. Horace's fellow Roman, Longinus, wrote a treatise *On the Sublime* which has had a long and influential history both amongst the eighteenth-century writers – Dryden, Addison, Pope, Goldsmith and Gibbon, and romantic writers – Burke, Goethe, Wordsworth, Coleridge, and Matthew Arnold; where sublimity was 'construed as the height of grandeur, nobility and generosity expressed as largeness and fineness of idea and feeling matched similarly by expression' (Harmon, *Classic Writings on Poetry*). The sublime was regarded as a key element in poetry. It is largely absent in twentieth-century poetry. Lucretius sought to advance the science of the day in his long poem *On the Nature of Things (De Rerum Natura)*. He developed Democritus's atomic theory, dispensing with the gods in human affairs, foreshadowing evolution and exploring the resultant Epicurean aspects of philosophy. And Virgil in the four books of his *Georgics* influenced many generations on aspects of agricultural, ecological and environmental issues. Issues which in our age are becoming globally urgent for survival, though largely unaddressed by our established poets.

Sir Philip Sidney in his *Apology for Poetry* repeatedly emphasised that the purpose of poetry was to 'teach and delight'. Poetry was to engage wisdom and imagination, and Sidney gave to it a high calling: the poet writes the particular truth but uses the imagination to draw from it also the general truth (unlike philosophers who deal only in general truths and historians who deal only with the particular). Shelley, in his *Defence of Poetry* argued that poetry 'marks the before un-apprehended relation of things' producing 'wisdom mingled with delight'. He states that the great instrument of moral good is the imagination, and that poetry makes immortal all that is best and most beautiful in the world. Now this may seem high-flown to modern ears. But it is most certainly a long way from T S Eliot's 'helpless moral anguish and emotional despair and paralysis', and Larkin's 'wan unhope' (David Perkins, *History of Twentieth Century Poetry*). As Larkin himself pointed out in relation to the idea that poetry can only be written out of suffering – 'there certainly is a cult', but: 'it's the big sane boys – Chaucer, Shakespeare, Wordsworth, Hardy – who get the medals'.

The careful and sober assessment of Wordsworth and Coleridge is illuminating. Wordsworth in his preface to the *Lyrical Ballads* stated that the aim of poetry was to give pleasure, which was partly done through the poem having a 'worthy purpose'. Here is Sidney's 'teach and delight' and Aristotle's claim that poetry is the most philosophical of all writing. Wordsworth thought the poet could achieve this by looking at the world in a spirit of love and by an acknowledgement of the beauty of the universe. 'Poetry is the breath and finer spirit of all knowledge'. But 'all knowledge' is exactly what the twentieth-century poets did not master. There is little science – physics, chemistry or evolutionary biology, little on the huge ramifications of globalisation, little engagement with the claims of formal religion or with the destruction of the world's environment proceeding at pace all around us, exacerbated by our huge and growing numbers. In short, the world as it actually is. All that has been left to the often excellent, but mainly lengthy, volumes of the prose writers of various disciplines, popular scientists, historians, geographers and so on.

'The poet binds together by passion and knowledge the vast empire of human society', said Wordsworth. He is often regarded as a 'nature' poet, but as a young man he was a political revolutionary, sympathetic to the French Revolution, and was subsequently engaged with the moral and national issues of the Napoleonic Wars, as in his sonnets on liberty. He was thoroughly aware of the scientific nature of his age. On science itself this 'nature' poet had this to say: 'If labours of the Man of science should ever create any material revolution in our condition the poet... will be at his side. The remotest discoveries of the Chemist, the Botanist or Mineralogist will be as proper objects of the poet's art as any upon which it can be employed.' Insights and territory largely abandoned by twentieth-century poets.

Matthew Arnold took his poetry very seriously as a 'moral teacher', for which he was sometimes mocked. His own style, in seeking 'high' poetry, tends to the archaic, but if you replace 'thou and thine with you and your' etc the poems can take on a new and contemporary interest. And in 'Dover Beach' he addressed one of the great issues of the day, the debate between science and religion. Partly because of globalisation, public religious and moral issues are now seen as worldwide and urgent. But the twentieth-century poets wrote for the most part about particular private experience.

Arnold's poem caught the unease of the times. In this area of the balance between reason and imagination, Housman, a classicist, is illuminating. He criticises eighteenth-century poetry, basically as too rational, at the expense of imagination.

But the combination of the two (he cites Shakespeare's 'Fear no more the heat of the sun'), he calls the summit of lyrical achievement. He also has high praise for eighteenth-century prose – which developed a 'workmanlike, athletic excellence greater than any before or since' – 'a trustworthy implement for accurate thinking and the serious pursuit of truth'. The poetry of twentieth-century poets (to speak in a broad generalisation) have seriously underplayed the use of reason in narrative and argument, and thereby sense, coherence and comprehensibility. They have often pursued instead a somewhat narrow band of personal psychological imagination, or a fragmented imagery, dissonances carried too far for reason or empathy to follow, or holding that the sound of the words alone, rather than their sense or meaning, is the poetry.

The historian, G M Trevelyan, in his essay *Religion and Poetry* says: 'Religion and poetry... in their higher manifestations... derive from a common origin in the spiritual and imaginative power of man, which forbids him to take a purely material view of the world, and gives him a glimpse of something to find, either external to, or immanent in, nature and humankind.' He remarks that some of our great poets were not religious-minded, but were men of the world. Chaucer's subject 'is the love of men and women not the love of God'. He argues that Marvell uses philosophical metaphors and images, but rather for poetical than for philosophical purposes and adds that he had 'a deep poetical sense of spiritual values, and of first and last things'. Trevelyan remarks that: 'It is the special function of secular poetry to give to ordinary human themes their full spiritual value, which the poet has the sensibility to perceive and the power to make his readers feel. Such, in particular, is the work of the greatest poet of all, Shakespeare.' But the support given by secular poetry to ethical enlightenment 'is given in the attitude towards right and wrong pervading poems that have no direct didactic purpose. In this way Shakespeare is a very great moral teacher.' He is seen as a true proponent of Sidney's 'teach and delight'.

With that background of what has historically been regarded as the higher purpose of poetry, I turn to an attempt to set out, in a short and probably inadequate form, a picture of our poetic scene in the twentieth and early twenty-first century in relation to such higher poetic aims. Again, in a short introduction this cannot be in any way a full critical account, but merely ideas and pointers.

Where to start? It could perhaps be further back, but let it be the eighteenth century, with its fusion and settling down of the Renaissance with the new science. Broadly, it enshrined reason and not natural emotions. It did so in its classically formal, reasoned style. But, importantly for the future of poetry, reason thereby became suspect. From this 'cage' of style and diction the romantic sensibility gradually released poetry, partly through 'emotion recollected in tranquillity', and established the role and profundity of nature in the life of humanity. It did so in 'natural', simple but imaginatively charged language – that of Chaucer, Shakespeare and the best of English tradition. Wordsworth tried to reconcile his view of the natural world with religion – a form of Christianity in his case – with limited success, because our understanding of biology had not then crystallised, but awaited Darwin and later evidence, such as the working of DNA. The knowledge is there now, but you would not know it from much twentieth-century poetry. This has largely continued to be written in the social-literary mode of poetry and subject matter; as if the profound scientific discoveries of the twentieth century, which changed and will further change mankind's view of the world and the wider universe, had never taken place. For poetry to regain its place, it must both reflect and inform that change.

Some attempts were made to grapple with this new-found world by some of the Victorian poets, for instance Tennyson and Matthew Arnold. But by then 'The grand idea of poetry as an all-embracing and unifying influence, irrespective of technical forms, had already been tacitly given up'. (Bayley, *The Romantic Revival*). The later Victorian poets had by the early twentieth century (Bridges and others) run dry, having exhausted, though in Tennyson's case always mellifluously, even reworked medieval romanticism. This twilight of an outworn mode, apart from a few fine late-flowering poems, is reflected in the Georgian poets.

Then came the near suicide of Europe in the First World War. Old certainties of superiority and empire were swept away. Brook's soldier gave way to Owen's horrified stare at the new reality. Yet Owen did so with 'Reason qualified by an ample romantic imagination' (David Perkins, *ibid*). The poems are memorable, accessible, and used for political purposes; another lesson that might have been a way forward for poetry, had Owen lived.

But then came Eliot, and Eliot I think was in considerable part responsible for much of the wrong turning poetry took for a long period of the century. The setting was this. After the murderous slaughter and destruction of the First World War it became clear that the old pre-war world was not returning. Instead there was social upheaval, civil war in Ireland, revolution and destruction in Russia, the sullen disintegration in Germany caused by the War and reparations, the Spanish flu killing millions, and the gradual realisation that the 'world fit for heroes' would not emerge in industrial society.

In this setting, in 1922, T.S. Eliot, who had married disastrously, had a nervous breakdown in the previous year, and had no religion at that stage to comfort him, produced *The Wasteland*; a poem that reflects the negativity in the world, but also promotes that negativity. *The Wasteland* was not simply a commentary on a dysfunctional world, but reflected a world seen through the filter of a frightened and appalled mind. You hear it in Eliot's own gloomy reading of *The Wasteland*. He was scared of life, and frightened of being thought a poser in his poetry. Hence his acceptance of Pound's savage editing and his own notorious and wilfully obscure footnotes, which have confused and confounded generations of young readers obliged to study the poem. Damaged by his upbringing and temperament – the debilitating uncertainty of a Prufrock – he watched the world with a doubtful smile, bemused by his own fame. He used his learning as a smoke screen and as a personal prop in a world he viewed as alien. He was too afraid of life to be a life-enhancing great poet in the mode of Shakespeare. He was of the troubled aspects of his age, but that is long past. *The Wasteland* remains a seminal landmark, but if it was the great modernist poem, and if it was also, as is often argued, the high point of modernism, then modernism was a very limited offering.

Because of Eliot's great influence through *The Wasteland*, his criticism and his gate-keeping of English poetry at Faber, he has for too long caste a restrictive influence over English poetry. Faber under Eliot published 'purist' editions of poetry, where the poems were usually printed with little information, about them or the poet, to help appreciation. And since Faber was the most influential main publisher of English poetry, the unhelpful format continued to discourage all but a relatively small band of poetry devotees. It is a great pity. Happily, in recent years the Faber format has broken out of this straightjacket and become increasingly helpful. In his poetry Eliot voiced an intoning of despair, and in the *Four Quartets* the only refuge he could offer was a retreat into an outworn form of religion and reactionary politics. This trend in the *Four Quartets* became even clearer in his religious plays, each of which is less good than the previous one. Eliot never explores the roots of religion, he merely adopts the poetic and incantatory in it. For those familiar with The King James Bible, which he often echoes, the poems acquire a status by association. But to others the poems are a mouthing of words, and an erudite disguise to conceal that the words mean very little. It is the equivalent of the high Victorian treatment of the Arthurian legends, and about as valid in present times.

His legacy? With *The Wasteland*, he made it impossible for the previous effete writing to continue as in any way serious poetry. That was a great service, and undoubtedly a major watershed. His important poems are difficult and obscure, and with partial exception of *The Wasteland* and a few others, of increasingly less relevance in the world. It is time for his reputation and influence to diminish. The world is too interesting and enjoyable a place for Eliot to have a big place in it. Poor Eliot. Even as a young man he tended to the miserable. He wrote: 'Cheerfulness, optimism and hopefulness; there stood a great deal of what one hated in the nineteenth century'. Poetry, he then felt could 'find its material only in suffering' Only? – tell that to some of our earlier poets. My poem 'The Trials of Poetry' may at least be read, as well as a severe critique of his influence, as a tribute to his vital contribution to modernising poetic style.

So what of other major twentieth-century poets? First there was Hardy, born in 1840: a nineteenth-century architect, turned novelist, turned latter-day poet. His romanticism was shot through with realism, which gave him a new voice, but sometimes a bitter one. He tried to rescue his better self from his difficult experience of life – hence the poems reflecting on his early love for his late wife, though the marriage itself was largely unhappy. But his bitter life-view limited his work – as in his view of malign fate in his novels and his Titanic poem, 'The Convergence of the Twain', which was more of a fatalistic myth than a reflection of the age of science.

In that he was close to early Yeats. Yeats himself had wonderful imaginative gifts ('Peace comes dropping slow'). When he had thrown off the myths and mists of Celtic mythology, and his flirtation with quasi-psychological replacements, he bought his gifts into the modern world. The late poetry is realist while retaining his imaginative power. Perhaps more of Yeats' work will survive than Eliot's. It is more life enhancing; another clue to poetry's way forward. There were other paths too – Frost and others renewed the pastoral from the supposed ruins of the twentieth century, a perception which accorded with the experience of many, hence Frost's popularity and influence. Like Yeats he forged a romantic realism and language to match. Houseman's 'Loveliest of Trees' and Edward Thomas's 'Adlestrop' are examples in the same mode.

But Hardy died in 1928 and Yeats in 1939, and other poets who promised much did not fulfil that promise. Auden's early work was more of the real world than much previous poetry – he had studied psychology and anthropology and had a scientific approach, enquiring and impartial. But Auden, whose poetry declined after the 1930s and Dylan Thomas, who flared wonderfully but briefly before snuffing himself out, had effectively left the scene by about 1950. After which, with honourable poetic exceptions amongst the many poets and attempted movements in poetry (some touched on below), there was a yawning gap. Fundamentally, a new age of poetry did not emerge. Rather, poetry as a central part of our literature and culture declined in influence still further.

There were of course many external reasons for this. In 1950 television in Britain was virtually unknown. Fifteen years later nine-tenths of households had television, and its dominance in terms of its coverage and intrusive influence in peoples' lives has continued to grow. And that was the beginning – there are the many developments of modern technology via computers and social media that have enticed the world away from more traditional forms of reading and culture.

But this decline is in part also down to the poets of the time. To many mainstream readers too much modern poetry seems more concerned with the inner struggles of the poet, than with providing pleasure for readers of poetry. A major danger of writing 'difficult' poetry, supposedly to reflect the age, is that it alienates the young, at school and afterwards. It thereby tends to destroy the base from which new poetry might appeal to and influence a wider public. Difficult issues do not justify opaque and obscure writing. Einstein's remark in a scientific context is salutary: 'If you can't say it simply, you don't understand it well enough.' We may still admire Coleridge's insight: 'Poetry gives the most pleasure when only generally and not perfectly understood.' But he was envisaging 'throwing the modifying colours of the imagination' over a poem of sense and reason. He also remarked that poetry is recognised 'as having more than usual order' and that 'good sense is the body of poetic genius'. He was not advocating incoherent poetry - a string of words and images for which meaning depends largely on whatever fancy and association the reader may attach to them; if indeed he or she can have the patience to do so at all.

By the 1970s, the most considerable poet to emerge in Britain was arguably Larkin. Like Yeats, he started doubtfully. His first book – perhaps through shyness or lack of confidence – was opaque, semi-comprehensible and of 'quasi realistic and quasi personal experience and wan unhope' (Perkins, *ibid*). Like Hardy, Larkin suffered from low-grade psychological depression. Within the limits he set himself, or which were set by his depressive life-view and background ('the object of writing is to show life as it is'), he wrote some fine realist poems combined with considerable imaginative strength. Like Hardy and Yeats, but few other English twentieth-century poets, Larkin's work continued to develop – his last two collections, *The Whitsun Weddings*, 1964, and *High Windows*, 1974, contain some of his best poems. But his expressed hesitant pessimism and restrictive view of life, as in 'Mr Bleany' always limits the possibility of wider success.

Other poets with reputations were Hughes and Heaney. But Hughes the countryman stayed mentally in Yorkshire. His better view of the connectedness of humanity with nature is found in particular in his poems about river fishing. Otherwise he largely focused on the bloody reality of nature's carnivores – red in tooth and claw – as in 'Hawk Roosting' and 'Pike'. He turned the nature of Wordsworth into a semi-incomprehensible dark cruelty, as in 'Crow'. To understand the beautiful, complicated development of life through evolution, you are much better served by the prose literature of the biologists. His biographer, Sir Jonathan Bate, thought his work on the mythical symbolism of animals was largely unreadable. And when he stepped out, it was into black magic and the paranormal; or the maelstrom of personal tragedy, guilt and self- justification in 'Birthday

Letters'. Poetry as an enlightening pleasure? No. Illuminating an age of extraordinary scientific and technological advance? No. He followed a twentieth-century obsession: that poetry is only made out of poets' troubles. And in the end, he abandoned it for his Iranian play and his unsatisfactory book on Shakespeare. He became more famous as a celebrity than for his poetry.

Heaney came from farming stock, and mentally for the most part, stayed in Northern Ireland. He started well – his poems on his farm experience as a boy caught a real poetic beauty. They engage with nature, but nearly always from the farming, human and personal perspectives, though simply and effectively rendered, as in 'Blackberry Picking' and 'Follower'. He was always aware of, but turned away from the disturbing cruelty in nature, as in 'Death of a Naturalist' and 'Barn'. Part of his later reputation rested on his being a decent man struggling to write of difficult times in Ireland; but he was never really a political poet - much of the work is puzzlingly oblique, as in 'Bogland', with its archaeological theme. And when he found himself lauded in a wider world it was perhaps in part because of the paucity of other contenders; and in the end he looked backwards, turning to translation – *Beowulf* and the *Aeneid*. That is fine, to keep alive and renew the stories, but does not advance our live poetry.

There is of course a new generation of poets, but it is perhaps too early to assess them objectively, and beyond the scope of this essay. And because of the diminution of poetry's place in educated society, much of it is published by small presses which struggle to catch the interest of a wider audience; much more remains unpublished despite the efforts of poets to place their work, and literary festivals to provide outlets through their competitions. But there is great hope in the range and opportunity in contemporary poetry, and the ways of disseminating it to reach the public.

So far, this brief excursion into the purpose and history of poetry has lacked the company of female poets. Look at any anthology of poems up to the mid-nineteenth century and you will find few female writers. In the past, women's poetry was largely unpublished and unknown, or remained unwritten, partly as a result of educational discrimination, and partly social and cultural expectations. This unhappy state of affairs gradually changed in the nineteenth century, aided and accompanied by the good work of female novelists. Enter the likes of Elizabeth Barrett Browning, Christina Rossetti and Emily Dickinson. Those relatively few became in the twentieth century a much larger number. And now in anthologies female poets are widely represented, and in poetry competitions probably half the poems are by female poets. They have social, sexual and economic freedoms unknown in earlier times; and with these come cultural opportunities and responsibilities. How successful and influential this influx of poetic power will be in the twenty-first century will depend on what poetry they write. But it is an exciting prospect for the new enhancement of civilised humanity.

In Britain it has been estimated that the overwhelming majority of people never read 'serious' poetry after leaving school. But despite the increasing cultural irrelevance of 'serious' poetry, there clearly is among the public a desire for some of the things that poetry has previously delivered. This surfaces in much popular culture. A great deal of modern poetry is written, but much of it is ephemeral or fragmentary and not easily understandable. But poetry in the form of performance art and 'sound' poetry has tried to fill the gap. This is often attached to a form of lyric in music. The best of it, such as Bob Dylan's lyrics, allied to his highly individual phrasing and arresting melodies has given pleasure to huge numbers of people, who sense a human, emotional take on the world. But very often in much pop, rock, rap and folk music the words are disjointed and highly repetitive. There are often many repeats of key phrases but little development and little attempt at establishing a coherent story or narrative; the lyrics relying rather on their signature phrases attached to a few notes of melody sufficient to raise and stir elements of emotion. Very often the words are of less importance than the beat of the music, against which the words can be largely inaudible. Such work can clearly have a wide appeal and, so far as it goes, has an important role.

But it only goes so far. It does not fulfil the central value of poetry as an informing and civilising culture. It will not provide a true or lasting way forward for poetry in the sense it has been largely understood down the centuries: 'the grand idea of poetry as an all-embracing and unifying influence' on civilisation. Something altogether greater is required.

In summary, a revitalised approach to poetry might include these elements: to write using a clear and realistic conversational language the aim of which is to give pleasure and understanding; a poetry in touch with a wide universal morality; broad in scope and subject; deeply personal in feeling and empathy. Add a sense of purpose and something of uplifting seriousness, but with the freedom of the whole laughing body and range of human kind trying to raise itself – as in the humanity of Chaucer and Shakespeare. In the plays, Shakespeare's poetry and moral outlook are embedded in wonderful stories: let us have our own narratives, and thereby a great deal of pleasure. How many kids at school nowadays learn to love poetry through stories, as the older generations enjoyed theirs, creating lifelong poetic loyalty, and a poetic base for their own times?

Let us acknowledge but not be restricted by much of the inchoate psychological frozen twentieth-century numbness, such as the 'emotional despair and paralysis' of Eliot's 'Hollow Men'. And rehabilitate reason in poetic language and imagination as 'a trustworthy implement for accurate thinking in the serious pursuit of truth'. We need a simple but imaginative directness. The constraints that hobbled so many twentieth-century poets need to be thrown off. Poets should be renaissance-like men and women – all knowledge should be our province – and once again leaders and makers of culture and society.

So, what should be the qualities of a poet? A person, Wordsworth said, who 'rejoices in the spirit of life, delighting to contemplate the goings on of the Universe, and habitually impelled to create them where he does not find them'; a long way from psychological misery and despair. Yes, the affairs of the world are too much out of joint. But the higher role of the poets is to be wise, knowledgeable, aspiring and wholly human, and through their art help to inform, heal, lift, entertain and make happy whatever sections of society in the world they can reach; which, with English as a world language and in an age of technological communication, should be many. This puts poets writing in English in a privileged but particularly responsible place.

You will see I have confined my remarks largely to English poets. I am acutely aware of this limitation. But a wider critique would be very large, beyond the scope of this little endeavour; though I think it true that much European and American poetry of the twentieth century suffers from the same limitations as English poetry. We have nearly all been subject to the partial destruction of our civilisation by military and ideological conflict, and saw it being rebuilt quite differently. As to the ancient and wide range of Asian poetry, from Turkey eastwards through the Middle East, Persia, India and on to China and the orient, I leave it to friends abroad, and any poets and scholars who may read this, to judge what part of my thesis may apply in the wider sphere of our world. But I hope the love and usefulness of poetry may thereby be extended; for we need it.

As well as great challenges, there is a great deal to be optimistic about in the world. Many millions of people live better lives materially and health-wise than ever before in history. In all cultures, poetry provides, or can provide, an enhancement of life. I hope the foregoing criticisms of English poetry may be a beneficial spur to the work of present and future poets who may come across them, and so enrich the lives of a widening range of our human family.

The Opening Stream

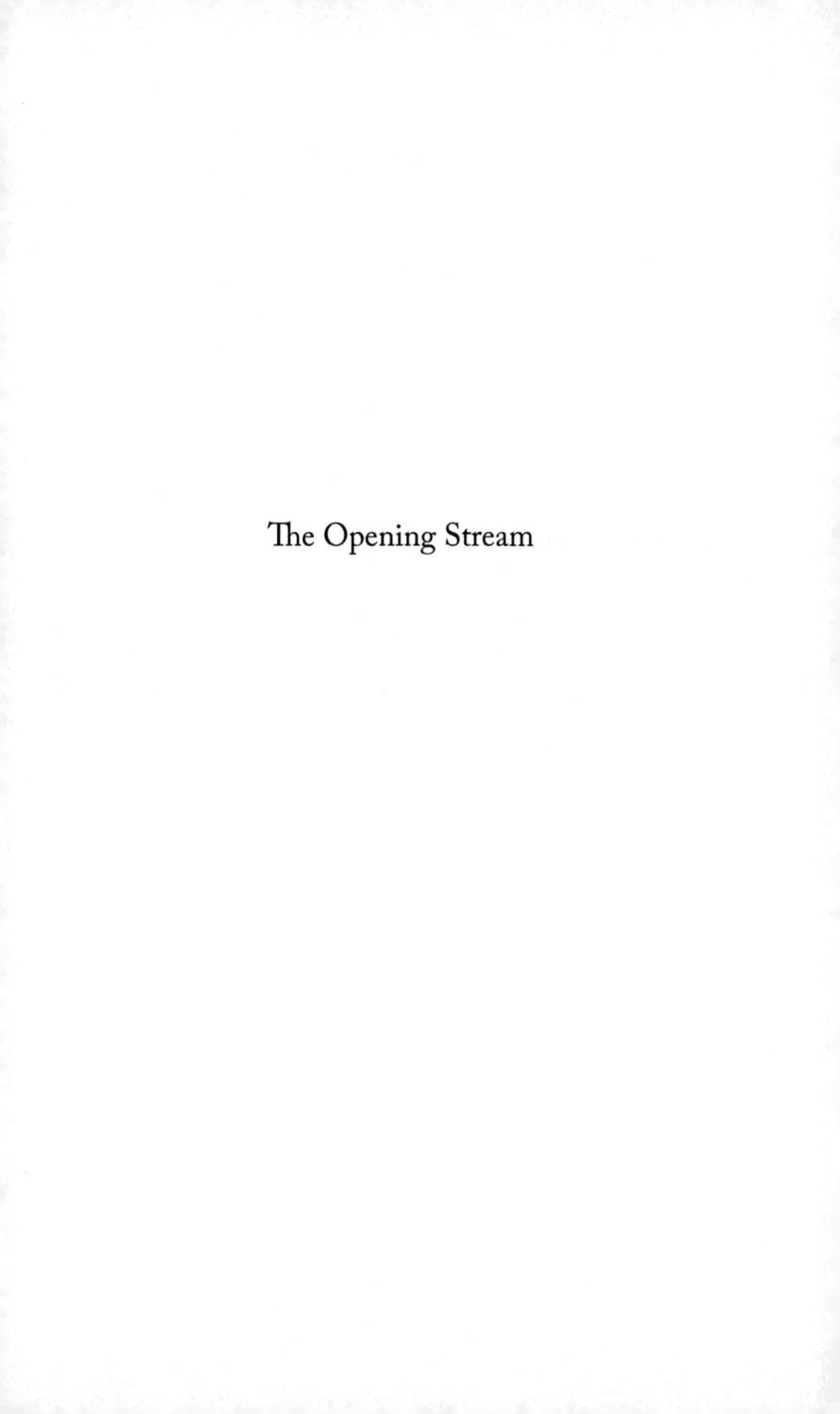

The Target

When I was a boy
I had a bow and arrow
And a straw-stuffed target
With ambition-tempting rings
Of bright alluring colours,
And at its heart, the gold;
And stood it proudly in a field.

Mostly the arrows
Ploughed the grass or flew beyond,
But on occasion
Hit the mark,
Boyish exhilaration rising then,
And Robin Hood heroic tales
Seemed, briefly, possible.

And then I aimed my arrows
At a girl, so beautiful,
Breath stopping when she turned her head.
I raised my bow, as young men will,
And loosed my arrows for the heart –
Exhilaration flowed again,
Eternal love and Shakespeare then
Seemed, briefly, possible.

Now I am old but bend my bow again,
For hope may triumph over
Expectation and distracting years.
Who knows? – the bull's-eye

May yet be within my range –
My hand is on the keyboard
And still I feel exhilaration rise;
So I will loose my arrows.

This Unassuming Beauty

From where did it come,
Her unassuming beauty?
Graceful of limb and line and glance –
I caught my breath in wonder.

So I sat a long hot summer afternoon
And watched, ostensibly, the tennis
From the shadow of an oak,
But all the while was watching
In delight the peace her presence brought.

I loved her then, but knew no way
To tell her of my love:
Too shy to take her by both hands
And say 'I love you'. She, so young,
Would shrink away: and I, so young,
Fearing rejection, and the jibes of others.

So I would not jar the idyll
Of a happy afternoon,
But hoped for future days and times;
And so I lost her.

What Shall I Feel?
a sonnet

What shall I feel if tomorrow is goodbye,
And I may not receive your kiss again,
Or gaze more in your sapphire-smoky eyes
Or know your perfume stealing through my brain?
For all things have their autumn soon or late,
And who can say if fortune will tomorrow
Wrap us close enfolded for a space
Of fleeting time, or mark a time of sorrow?
Why then, times come would soon be times gone by,
And I would have these few poor lines to show me
That I did not dream, nor my memory lie,
Remembering you as soft as drifting snow
And all the hundred yous I have not sung,
But lived with for a while when we were young.

The Student's Dilemma

Did I spread myself too thinly?
Interesting diversions lured me on –
In history, some philosophies,
In art, religion, politics
Music and literature;
Each one of which to minds more formed
Was in itself a world, a universe.
And I loved too the natural world we also walked –
The rivers, grasses, hills, islands, the sea, the mountains –
All – and the girls and friends I knew.
We shared the exploration of our worlds.
The endless possibilities of youth were ours.
I thought that time and life were limitless.

Salute to the Cinema

How when, with noise and pain, the drudgery
Of work is done, how many dull hard lives
Creep out in best rag scarf and drab black coat
To join the throng of young, (pink lipstick, slim white tie
And flashy suit) upon the paper littered pavement.
How then they find their queues to happiness
Outside the Regal, Astor, Metropol.
For them some fair young form will smile
And share her dazzling technicolour world
With rows of weary, plodding human kind.
Old mothers see their past glad days return
In full warm flood; they laugh, are sad, see fine
Bright loves, are lifted from their daily lives
To cherish other worlds than theirs
To savour happiness, or tears,
For some brief evening that may stay
In thought for weeks, perhaps for months, to come.
And after climb in hard iron beds, rest happy, think
A while, sigh in the dark with peaceful eyes –
So fall asleep, perhaps to dream new life –
Before the dawn brings back the sober day, renewed.

Town Bands in Germany

One summer as I hitchhiked from the Alps,
Those German towns along the Rhine
From Basle to Heidelberg
Shone in the sun, their old stone streets
Loud to the thump of town-band marches.
Brassed tunics bobbed through red-roofed squares,
The women waved, the children ran,
The colours were bright and bold.
I felt a strong proud people stirring
In Germany that day.
But some did not see those colours,
Nor heard the happy sounds,
But dimly they saw massed ranks of grey
With the red white black flags floating,
And they heard the tramp of heavy-shod boots,
The sweeping roar, and the grimly rumbling tanks.
I saw some there, remembering,
Turn in silence from the scene.

Weather and Authority

Philip of Spain, God's emissary on earth
Built galleons for the glory of his cause
And with proud ceremonial prayed to God
For weather and for holy victory.
But God, it seems, had planned for gales,
And took the English side,
Or so they said; at least they knew the Channel storms,
And when to run for port,
While poor Sidona, sumptuously cabined,
But sick within his heaving bed,
Could only dream of orange groves in Spain.
And all the end of that endeavour was
To pour away near half the New World's gold;
And spend the lives of Spanish sailors,
Who never saw the southern sun again,
Except a few, who left a scattering
Of dark-eyed children down the Irish shores.

Napoleon saw his glory spreading to the east.
And took his brightly glittering troops to Muscovy
Across the summer plains and pliant rivers.
He did not pray to God (some said
He secretly believed he was a god).
But he forgot to take his winter clothes,
And found he did not like the Moscow winter cold,
Nor Moscow burning, nor the stubborn foe.
So slunk off home, mocked by the snow
And ice and freezing winds
Which were the death pall of Imperial France,
And killed six hundred thousand French troops on the way,
The all-engulfing snow their winding sheet.

A hundred years went by and then
The Emperors of Europe quite forgot –
Their pride and steel-clad national rivalry
Confounding all their judgment –
That rain and clay and shells in Northern France
In wintertime mean mud.
Three Emperors and a King, in most imperious
Highly polished boots, got stuck in mud,
Of one sort or another, which sucked their Empires in,
And killed four million sons of Europe.

Invaders always see the land in summer
When the weather's light and bright.
And so the Führer sent a million
Of the master race to Russia
And saw the dust clouds of his armour rolling on
Across the plains to open up his living space,
And, to the south, the oilfields of his dreams.
Five million Russian soldiers died for this.
But winter came and deadly cold
Crept all across the steppes, then bitter wind
Swept shrieking in, and all was lost for this:
That proper clothes were not on Hitler's list.
And so they froze and died, so many, many thousand
German young, in hasty shallow graves
Scrapped in the frozen earth so far from home.
For weather does not answer to authority.

Springtime in a Coppice

Just now I felt as Tolstoy felt
Among his springtime woods of Russian birch.
I looked up through the sunlit hazel twigs
At the blue white- scudding sky
And wondered that bare little twigs
Should after winter frosts and freezing winds
Produce this host of yellow-fluttering catkins
To make renewal in the northern world, and me.

The Cuban Crisis

Did you hear the message that was flashed
Round the world today?
It voiced threats and moves of war.
The peoples stirred uneasily,
And then, appalled, fearful but impotent,
The world waited tensely by radios,
Dreading to learn by sudden silence
Of the work of one man's word.

And I, barely coming to manhood
Thought bitterly over the scene.
I, who had laughed in my boyhood
Stood faced by an end of all the life,
Which my knowledge, gathered slowly over
Half-lit years, was opening up before me.
They could not war! – how dare they think
To contemplate the thing – what, national safety? –
To make our planet but a twisted wreckage,
Bearing a shattered, mutilated life – if one at all?

I saw the links of fatherhood stretching
Far back in the past. All things, all thoughts, condemn –
Damn, damn their reckless politics, this monstrous gamble –
I want to marry, to have a wife to love,
Beget fair children, see their children…
So rest in age, smiling at the passing of my time.
Ruminations and anger, inadequate thoughts
As we waited, waited, upon an anxious day.

A Student's Turmoil: Careers, Life and Love

Can I love the shadow of a girl I never knew?
What are the secrets of the mind
That now, a long and calmly different year
Since last I saw her,
She should still delight me so?

What makes a man to love?
Some may know themselves, not I.
I did not know, and did not guess
Beyond what I was taught,
Where the deep stirrings come from.
All was veiled and left untold.

I lived two lives, the student in the Oxford term,
With laughter, punts and teas in rooms.
But all the time within was seething struggle
Threatening to engulf the person who is me.

I see her sitting on the lawn,
But she only casts a passing eye on me;
I turned cut off from knowing her
By the rising ceaseless tumult in my mind.

Alone, alone you fight. You hear advice
From friends and tutor, see their jaws
Go up and down, hear their well-intentioned words,
And argue, thank, agree to stop them talking.

But after these, the unreal interludes,
Alone again you turn to fight anew
The same relentless issues
That block the road of love, careers and life.

Until one day, with teeth still clenched
And aching muscles tensed for the next assault,
I found the silence of the lonely victor –
Career, and love decisions made –
Who does not yet believe
That there will be no more renewed attacks,
Or that the weary months are conquered.

And now, a long year later,
In the progress of an ordinary life,
She comes to me as free and close
As someone who has always stood beside me.

By some perplexing trick of time
Through all those silent heaving months
And scattered social meetings,
Did we, by unknown and unspoken means,
Somehow draw closer?
But though I still don't know what lies beyond,
I smile and wonder if our eyes will now meet differently.

Forebears and Descendants

I am not me; yet I am me – a conflux
Made of genes – my father's and my mother's, quarter each;
Four grandparents – a sixteenth each;
A quarter from remoter pasts –
Some little bit a nameless girl
My great-great grandpa knew.
Shall I survive? Within this conflux, briefly,
Before my genes and molecules disperse.
Ten couplings on and my descendants then
Shall be one thousandth (only that) of me.
Therefore I will not fret at seeds of life or death
For they are but the start and end of life,
And life itself is how I live and love
In the rolling present of my gifted days.

We Were Gods

We were gods in the mountains that day.
And talking of strange notions, I became
As one who feels some old familiar truth revealed,
As if the shackles of our purblind life
Were shaken off and lost below us in
The valleys of the mist. And opaque facts
Became translucent, revealing connotations
From new concepts now perceived,
Becoming things of preternatural beauty of themselves
And echoing wide significance afar.

We stood in starlit night upon the lonely moor
Imbibing such a beauty from the dark
Clear light as made the scene of garish day
Seem circumscribed and flat.
There love stood laughing, well-be-known and free,
Reality was found a thing of joy –
Chaos and order smiling side by side,
Well understood, acknowledged, wondered at,
And truth did triumph of her own,
Under the restful motion of the earth.

A Seabird's Life and Death

A bird sits unavailing on its nest
And does not know defective eggs will never hatch,
And watches nests on nearby ledges
Reveal their chicks, and down turn into feathers.
And still she sits uneasy with her mate,
Blocked in that most urgent animal desire
To be fulfilled as a channel
Of the beauty of her species.

For this are feathers preened, fur licked,
Coats and colours annually renewed,
Before one day a crumpled pile of feathers
Or of fur, eaten out and gradually decayed,
Mark what was once a hope of life.

Some say the worst disaster
Is a failure of the line. It has been said
That children are the messengers we send
To times we shall not see,
And if that shall not be
The cries of unborn children sometimes haunt the years.

So we must build distracting shields –
Some other purpose greater or mundane –
To guard our guttering flame
And let us live within our little pool of light
Before the winds of time snuff us out too.
Thus this: a small act of defiance
To let me live and contribute a trifle to my race
Against the stopping of the genes;
A consolation no poor seabird has.

I Felt the Challenge

I felt the challenge of that Galilean Jew –
God, or man? He would not leave me well alone,
But dogged my day-thoughts in the London rush,
And where I turned, he was.

How can that fellow from a dusty shore
Follow me, follow me, down the underground?
All thoughts I followed, he sat at the end;
And yet I could not reach him; nor he me.

So is it true – of he who I was taught is God?
They say he is the living universal love.
But does such love demand submission, obeisant worship even?
And when I question, pride they say at once, is heinous sin.

And yet I think it is not pride, this strange
Developing resistance, but something deeper:
First questionings among the certainties,
The contradictions pushed aside as mystery, unanswered.

Then reasoning from a wider world, new truths perhaps,
And different truths, just glimpsed, but strongly felt, neglected.
If faith requires surrender and an end of exploration,
Then to my surprise perhaps our ways are parting.

After Glandular Fever

I sit upon a box marked 'NZ Meat' –
It came to us with Chris' old accordion
Packed inside, and spent all winter round the back
By the clump of winter iris.

I sit and rock from edge to edge,
Taking a breather from my books,
My strength returning in the warming sun.
And pivoting to quiz the sky

I catch the coming messages of spring
In the cold bright air of March.
Straw in the beaks of fluttering sparrows,
Wingings, twitterings of garden birds

And countless breathing, breaking signs
Of coming leaves, and blossom on the prunus tree,
And from the earth the spikes of daffodils
Pushing upward into life.

The box is weathered on three sides.
When winter comes we'll knock it up,
Maybe, for kindling wood;
But now it is a throne.

How can I work?

How can I work for my exam, cruel girl,
When laughing images of you distract me by the hour?
When you appear before my mind, books, laws,
Rules, cases, precedents dissolve
Into senseless reams of print.
Leave me alone, tempting and heartless one,
And if you will not let me be your love,
Then let me be a poor successful lawyer.
Now go. And don't come back again
Until I give you leave;
In half a minute's time.

Hope and Sadness

I sit alone, my love, and write to you
Of hope and sadness at your going:

Sadness because all things, at some time, pass,
And this may prove the slipping of our ties;
When you, like the bright-red-painted north sea ship
Moving away through the lower pool,
Dwindles down the broken warehouse channel
To silent homage from the mourning cranes,
And leaves all London desolately grey.
Then I am left, like the ageing piles
Of the wharf, empty and bereft of purpose,
Waiting, knowing that you may be detained
In reaches far from mine.

Hope because, poor humans that we are,
We love but rarely; and have lit
Our lanterns to each other in the dark.
There may be seas and slowly turning months,
My love, between us now; but steadily
We'll close, as two companionable boats,
Driven apart in darkness by the storm
Sail on alone at daybreak, expectantly
To find each other's course converging,
And in fulfilment of that hope
Laugh to see once more the well loved
Sail appear on the horizon; until the two,
Running together as if they shared one helm,
Ride into the quiet waters of their sound,
Homeward to rest.

Topography of Love

We are two resting lovers on a bed,
Two lovers breathing quietly side by side.
We feel each for the other's hand
Which there begins again an intertwining of our worlds.
Your beauty lies stretched out
Upon your back, the gentle curving wolds
Of rising softness, your landscape's shapely mounds,
My hipbones proud above my stomach's flat
And gently undulating plain,
Rising by a scarp slope to my ribs.
We turn our heads and link our eyes
And soft desire rolls each towards the other,
Plains and hills turned vertical by nature's force,
Seamlessly united, like close-fitting continents
Before tectonic plates move them apart,
Before the splits of time prise us apart.

I Sent my Love

I sent my love the image of a heart,
Symbol, twin halves united, of love's reign,
And on it did entwine like lovers' thoughts
A monogrammatic weaving of our names.

Let these poor figures celebrate our love,
Linking what we in life would link, so we,
If we're no longer intertwined in life
May live together by this imagery.

What Shall I Say?
a sonnet

What shall I say when you are worn and old?
Which daily turning of the world may bring
And your soft beauty's vanished on the wing
And people, of my love for you being told,
Say, this proves lovers to be led blindfold,
Bound in delusion, seeking heaven, sold
To insubstantial beauty, then disguised
By nothing but the error of their eyes.
I shall not waste my breath in hot denial
Or be extravagant in praising you,
For words of mine could not acquit that trial
Or any words establish youth anew.
But if a child of yours survived as proof
That living testament would mark the truth.

I Shall Not Praise This Greece

I shall not praise this Greece beyond her due,
Or say her state is always steady-helmed.
But she is beautiful: a sea-surrounded realm,
White marble isles set in her seas' deep blue,
Her white-bleached mountains rising in blue skies
Above her silver shimmering olive groves,
Where patient walls hold stony soil confined,
And sun-born fruits and bougainvillea-mauves
Blossom and flourish by the whitewashed walls
Of simple houses set down by the shore,
In dappled olive shade, or where the hillside falls
To the quiet-hushing sea of evermore.
Men long have said her beauty has no peer:
But it's not true: I've seen you walking there.

Shakespeare's England

Mud and shit in the gutter and orange peel from Spain,
But scarlet hose and jewelled swords pass by,
And in half-timbered taverns from an earlier time,
Discussion and philosophy: a new age talked into the world.

In ill lit rooms new palaces are built in minds
That range beyond the horizons of the sun.
In the revolutions of the stars – new worlds,
And in the teeming skulls of men – new worlds.

Freedom slowly won from superstition-stifling lives,
And freedom from religious wars that loom in Europe –
A freedom roughly imposed on England by the Queen,
Who now grows old and desiccated;

But who took her parliaments and people
To Acts of settlement that won precarious peace,
A peace in which her enterprises flourished –
Patents, trademarks, copyright and plays,

And parish poor law, piracy and trade.
Protected by the guns of little ships
And the sailors of her realm,
She thinking foul scorn of interfering kings.

Small wonder words blazed in the minds of men and poets,
Who set down wide humanity as never done before,
So all the world was in the playhouse,
And all of London learned there of the globe –

Seeing brave lives in ancient Greece and Rome,
Egypt, France and the half-myth city-states of Italy
And magic isles set in unknown seas, their
Princes, kings, fair ladies from past realms and new,

Lovers, wretches, jokers, boys and girls alike
Glittering, loving and dying in a little time.
And England ever after outward turned,
And future lives around the world were changed.

The Broader River

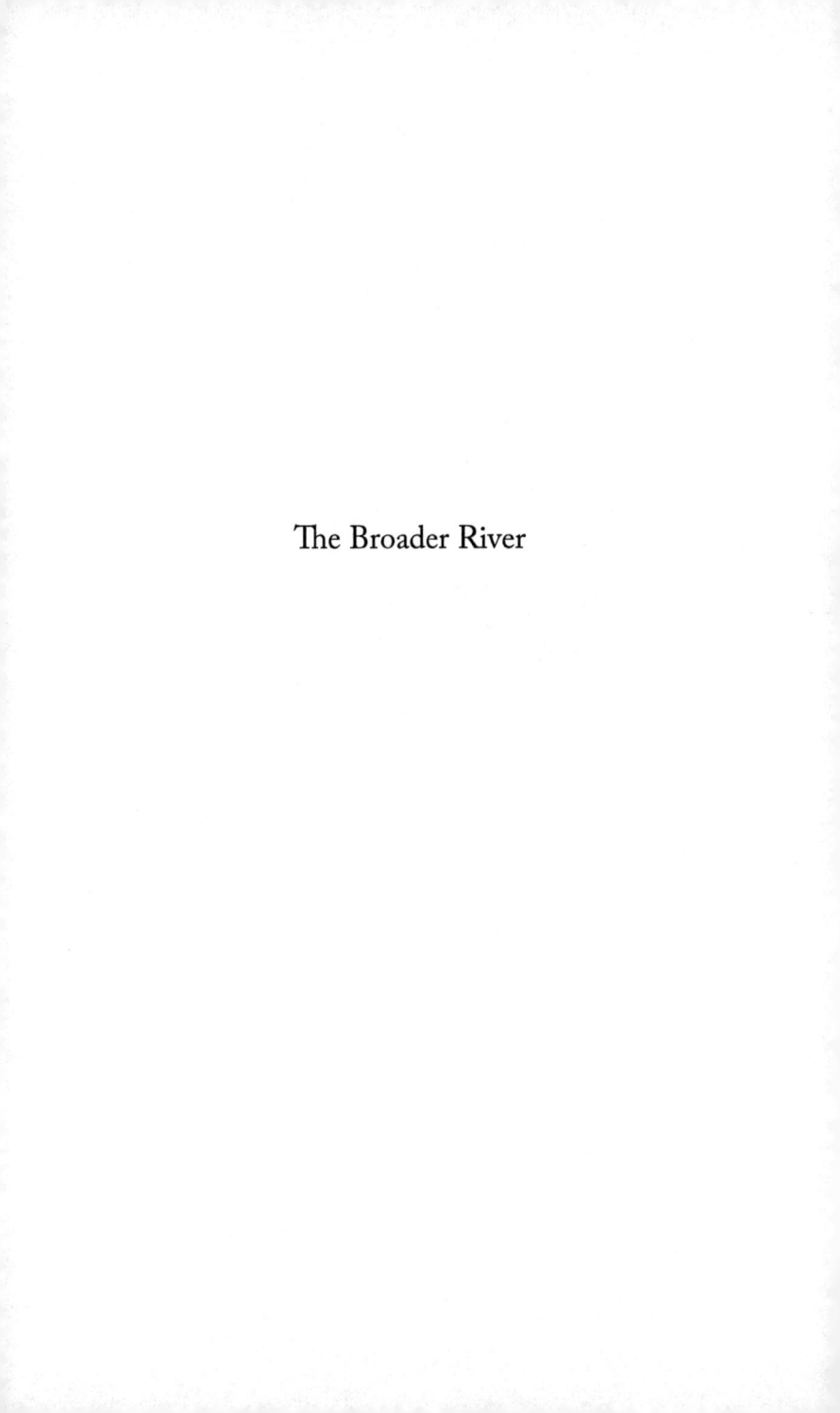

In Persia, 1974

I do not wish to go to Pasagardae:
That should be done in spring
When the flowers bloom across
The low-hilled plain where Cyrus
Set white palaces, and lined his gardens'
Purling water-courses with white marble;
But now a dusty yellow plain in summer.
Cyrus the Great, conqueror of half the then known world.
A poly deist, provider of religious freedom
Through his spreading lands.
A man it seems who sought to rule
With justice for his peoples,
Who lies beneath a simple stone memorial,
I hope in peace, in the plain of Pasagardae.
Therefore I think in hope of that first empire
As a template for the present state, Iran.

Shah Abbas the Great, Islamic lord of Persia,
Planted his city in the purple-mountained plain
And channelled qanats bringing water
Deep below that dusty land,
To reach its heart, and made the city green.
He brought skilled craftsmen from the Christian west
To help him build: decreeing that
They first should build their churches in his city.
Then he built the blue and golden mosques,
The wonder and the beauty of the age,
And palaces of delicate delight, where flowers
And song-birds still adorn the ceilings:
It is the dream of Persia, Isfahan.

But in Tehran
The ministers are mostly cynical
And word is everyone's corrupt,
Except the Shah.
Some of the younger ministers
Retain ideals, though they have seen
Graft and greed at work,
Syphoning the wealth of oil
That should help build a nation.

The hotel porter said, 'Yes, with the oil
We're rich; but who gets all the money?'
Certainly I know, down by the Caspian,
Along that favoured flowery shore, the ministers,
High civil servants, doers for the crown,
Receive rewards of parcelled lands
And handsome houses; yet who but they
Will build this land anew
In peace and wealth and toleration?

Here in Tehran the favoured live
Among the houses higher on the hill.
But in those fine apartments, newly built,
Cool marble-floored and lovely carpets strewn,
The silk ones glowing on the walls,
Signed photos of the Shah's chief minister,
They say, are disappearing overnight,
And anxious visits with strained smiles
Try to check the latest fall. That is the talk at least,
Though nothing in the press presages any fall.
'No, no, only junior ministers are being changed';
But everyone talks quietly, looking round.

Higher up the hill, the summer palace stands.
Within, a Cyrus? – planning for his people's future,
With care and warily, a liberal edging westward,
Or a ruthless spy-backed autocrat?
Neither will please the Mullahs. And the people?

I sit upstairs in a coffee shop,
A sign in English at the door, but in Farsi
Halfway up the stairs and at the top,
Windows open to the noisy street.
I feel the dry wind blow
In afternoon Tehran, and watch
The pale dust-covered leaves rustle in the lines
Of roadside trees. Beyond, some larger trees
Behind a high but somewhat crumbling wall,
Within, the watching British Embassy.

Outside the window on a dusty neon sign
I see a small dove sit,
Casting his head this way and that
To look by turns in at my window,
Then back towards the passing traffic.
Poor bird, how can that little head
Contain enough to understand
What that bright eye perceives.
It walks a step, the wind blown
Feathers ruffle. Little bird,
How can you understand? Can we?
Like you I, sometimes, am afraid.

Thank You Letter to the Poets

I joined a man on pilgrimage,
Laughing as he went along
The road of human kind.
He opened up bold lives and minds,
And newly shaped the language of our verse.

I knew a youth in London streets,
Larking as he quilled in verse
The lives and loves he lived and read,
New stories teeming in his head,
And spun in plays that made the world our own.

I heard a dark-haired Devon boy
Calling with his friend
'Follow us, follow us
And we will show you wonders here
That you will never see elsewhere',
And they led us into nature's ways.

The Trials of Poetry

Thomas Stearns Eliot, of various abodes,
Poet, is before us;
Yet still disguised and shrouded
By the concentrated folds
Of his much praised and intricate obscurities:
So cognoscenti use strange lenses to magnify his images,
Gathering the out of joint, the fractured and the scattered:
His standing thus enlarged beyond his stature.
A man of paradoxes,
For whom at the tolling bell
Time runs sandwards, unfolding backwards,
Meeting or perhaps not meeting at
The still turning point of somewhere out of time
Where past and future meet the present
Through a garden door he did not go
Where jumbled images of loss crowd in,
Symbols and cymbals, sounds and flickers, signifying

A phrase here, a fragment there
Shored up against an unknown fear
Dabbed at with words and phrases that repeat
Or half repeat the atrophy of desiccation and decay
In the dissolution of illusion and allusion,
Glinting with snatches gleaned from other lands –
Temps perdue, uber alles, morté, shards
Or shades of Dante Alegeira and some other bits
To counterpoint his high profanity:
Mass condemnation of dead people in dead towns, dead lands,
Who broke the imagined mould of Hellas in his mind.

In his beginnings we do not see beginnings
But maypole dances, hints of civil strife –
A sort of past recalled into the present
In which he then inserts the underground
And various modern terms – the Stock Exchange
And company directors – to tell us of the start of time.
And he is here or there or somewhere else
In his beginnings.

And what you do not say is the only thing you say
Changing the mode and syntax as you go –
As introducing 'I' in places, the seeing eye
With which he saw or thought he saw or didn't,
And trundles out that trick of paradox, as –
Time is, or is not, runs sideways, backwards,
Up or down and sometimes inside out:
Fancies filled with emptiness of meaning.

And then abruptly turns to verse
For fear of writing something worse,
On even comprehensibility,
And hides in rhymes
His splintered times
And his meaning ill defined, defined,
And his meaning ill defined.

A poet with a broken lute
In a nightmare once I saw
It was an ash-choked dirge he sung
As from his tortuous mind were wrung
Fragments from Mount Abhorrent.

He sowed confusion from behind
His tightly buttoned waistcoat
And his strictly slicked-down hair.
His watery smile became a leer
Because he could not understand
Why critics claimed what he had done
When he had done, but left his art obscure.

Thomas, we are abused:
For fear constrained you and your art
And fame and pride then silenced you.
And fear has never made a poet great.
So backwards then you went,
Retreating into old times lost.
Forwards, for us, you wrote no more,
Thomas has writ no more.

This much is true:
He freed the language from a worn-out mode
(And that will be his lasting monument);
But built a cage inside a cave for poetry instead,
And sat inside and turned his collar up
Against the gathering dark, mouthing
Incantations against the mess he saw,
Seeking to light an old and blood-flecked candle stub
To shine somehow against his fetid, dreary,
Worn-out image of the world.
His quatrefoil is four times foiled,
For in the world it marks a failed apotheosis;
And withered is the garland on the brow.

Backwards he went through the land of erudition,
To dry bones in the desert sand
Humming in the wind, fleshless and desiccated.
Where is the water to put on flesh again?

In a narrow well, crimped and clogged and silted up;
A mere drain, though here and there he found
A notable cracked stone bearing the markings
Of some far glimpse of things once better.
Better, to repeat, repeat the echoed echo
From the burned out charred remains
Of obscure years and cultures long decayed.

He only saw the second law
And did not know the others,
And did not look beyond his cave,
Save inwards at his flickering memories,
And saw a turgid river, and a fog-filled sea.
He never saw a sunlit shore
Or the great ocean rolling all before
Or the sunrise of renaissance in the earth.

I would not and I cannot harm the dead.
But the dead hand should not command the tiller,
And poetry must once again be free.

In the City, Seminars

In the City, seminars, admin arranged
By East End girls in well-paid jobs
And bright red lipstick, eyebrows plucked –
The bloody mascara's got into me eyes –
Who monitor the changing of the world.
We've got one coming up on electronic commerce.
What's that then, Kev?
Only the mode whereby the world economy accelerates
Beyond the dreams of Adam Smith –
Instant continuous free trade round the globe
By treaties, pacts and deals,
(The seas, the mountains, time and languages,
The passport-guarded nation states
All rendered obsolescent),
So electronic trade may flow in arteries
And veins and trickle through capillaries,
The swift and silent flow,
The lifeblood of the body commerce.
And gurus here give lectures on
The newest form of global trade for goods and services –
Digitalised production, online terms of trade
Systemic risk, encryption keys
And legal recognition of the latest electronic signatures.

Then lunch: cold finger buffets, and chicken
This or that, and wine. Kevin: *It gets them in,*
But use the smaller glasses, and don't emphasise the labels.
Bulgarian? Never 'eard of that.

Yes, much improved – and still dead cheap.
Got to keep the profit margins up, my girl –
And anyway they've got their heads in electronic clouds.
Cor – laugh a minute really.

And after lunch cross border data flows
Industrial privacy, definitions of protected works
And harmonising laws and tax
And government views on electronic tax environments
And whether to be or not to be conglomerates.
Amending Acts, de-furring arteries
And all that mighty heart pumping data
Via the satellites, minutely nuanced
And controlled by exceptions to exceptions
To exceptions, from statutory sub-clauses
Down to the smallest syllable of recorded regulations.
Cor blimey. 'ave they finished? That's it then. Let's go down the pub.

All Those Grey Solicitors

All those grey solicitors
Heading up to Town,
Home counties men –
Successful, most of them would say.
Daily up to Town they go
For long hours at the toil and comfort
Of their well-appointed desks.

That suave but balding gentleman,
Who likes his pricy chateau wines,
Is he aware that week on week
And year on year
He gives his living hours
To sort the tax affairs of richer men
And slowly, slowly casts his life away
In a mass of second-rate concerns?
Is he seduced by earnings and the wealth he sees,
Imprisoned by his four-star fence,
So says he cannot yet retire?
When did he last look at the stars,
And does he know he creeps towards his grave?

Fortieth Birthday

In forty years, when you and I are past
Our prime and old, perhaps we'll look back then
To this November time,
When forty winters *have* besieged your brow,
And we think now that youth has fled us –
But then we will look back and laugh to think
How young we were at forty.

New Year's Eve Party

Behind the jollity and chatter –
The party was on New Year's Eve –
(*More wine? Some food? Have you met Judith?*
My leg is killing me. Sit here)
I heard the iron gate of time clang shut.
The year had gone and we were shunted on
The other side. The place where I had lived,
The land of nineteen ninety-six, had gone;
And with it gone the opportunities
That only could be taken there.
What now was left undone could nevermore
Be done in that familiar place,
And all were thrust, though unaware and laughing,
Into a new space, a little smaller
Than the one we'd left, it's end still hidden,
But marked out. Beneath the fun all life became
More urgent in the ceaseless beat of time.

The Princess

High in the sunlit castle sang the bird
Her thrilling song brought joy to all.
The dazzling feathers and the flash of colour
Beloved of all who lived beneath the castle walls.

Her singing went through all the castle rooms
And long she sang to please her prince;
But she was unregarded by her prince,
And in a golden case was kept.

Attempted flights did not release the bird
And drooping feathers told her love-lost tale,
And death came rudely and the singing stopped
And all the castle folk and those below, grew pale and silent.

Since By My Age

Since, by my age,
I have no choice,
But must write now
Or die my thought
And song unsung –
I shall aim to
Be like Verdi
Composing some
Good work late,
So smiling in the face
Of my time's closure.

Two Universes

Copernicus believed the Earth went round the Sun
Displacing man from his pre-eminence.
And so it does; but now I also see
The centre of the universe for me
Is me – through me the world is lit:
I cannot see or hear but through these eyes and ears
Translated by the inner sanctum of my mind,
That wonder world of electronic messages and life.
The myriad pulses of the universe beat gently
In my brain and conjure god-like powers
Of wide-held images, beyond the scope
Of Galileo's lenses, and across the range of time.
And by this gift of language words and print
I can send my little signals out
Towards a time that I shall never see.

Four Fires

They say that fire,
Colossal force-filled fire,
Commenced the universe.
And vast in scale beyond imagining
Explosive fires – ten million million miles
Would not begin to measure –
Become for us, by distance,
Little dots of light
Sprinkled across the heavens.

And here below our feet,
Englobed beneath the fragile crust
Of plates and continents,
The remnants of that great primordial burst
Simmer and glow
And on volcanic days remind us so
With fiery savagery that startles us anew.

But then I know that love
Will light internal fires –
A lovely face and limbs conveyed
Into the mind, sending a pulse of fire –
Deep through my loins, my gut
Enveloping my heart –
An all consuming blaze
Lighting infernos of delight and sorrow.

For things burn out: that is
The nature of transforming fire: consume and change.
Bonfires of a summer garden's beauties

Gone to autumn and decay
Change all to ashes.
Our pyres of wood and gases changing us –
One will consume my body,
This vehicle of me, my loyal friend,
This lifeline of existence, that makes me possible
Across my span of years -
Marked only by a little heap of ashes
And the memories of others.

Time

That the speed and spectrum-place of light is known
Allows our minds
To find that light cannot exist
Outside of time
For, to exist, light has to travel;
And light takes time to pass.

So: no light outside of time
And so no visualised eternity
Or heaven; no heavenly choirs
(For sound is silent too except within
The moving space of time).

And all then turns on this:
What is the nature of that
Strange thing, time?

Sleep

Our own aurora borealis, veils of sleep,
Descending, dropping through
The hundred billion cells that galaxy our brain,
So closing up that miracle of consciousness
Through which we can recall all things
From furthest memories of childhood,
Sixty years or more ago, the images retained,
And all of that, resting in an electronic womb,
Sheltering by sleep the possibility
Of thinking life, and all imagination.

Heavenly Physics

Underneath Sir Isaac's wig
Celestial bodies spun
And from his speculation came
The order of the planets and the sun.

But Einstein had another thought,
And peered inside the atom,
And found that things did not add up
The way that had been taught.

The third part is unfinished yet
For those two can't agree.
So where's the mind that unifies,
And what will be the key?

He postulates some startling things:
That time is older than we thought,
And so space larger, and unmeasured;
That strings are loops of energy, not strings;

That gravity is both of pull and push;
That voids do not exist – dark matter fills all space;
And all the universe has only five dimensions,
Of time, of frequency, and the three of place;

That everything within the universe
Is energy – electro magnetism – in some form,
And gravity is therefore on that spectrum,
While time runs ever forward, never the reverse.
Thus unity achieved, and physics newly born?

On the Nature of Luck

Robed Seneca held luck to be
The meeting of preparedness
With opportunity.

My mother, who had faith in God,
Held no such thing as luck exists,
And all is ordered and ordained.

Now I have tested both in life,
It seems to me that she was wrong
And Seneca more right.

Victoria's Vespers
*about Tomas Luis de Victoria, a great Spanish
composer of the sixteenth century*

Victoria's Vespers,
Rarefied, certainly,
Written in faith,
In the face of a dark
And little comprehended world.

This music lit and held by
Candlelight against deep-shadowed
Echoing recesses,
The sound slow-pulsing
Through delicate stone pillars
With light reflected edges,
The audience still and silent.

The eternal rise and fall of sound,
The tryst of sacred music seeking God,
Of medieval wonder turning
To the new renaissance world,
With all its unknown coming changes,
And ignorant of what lay then beyond.

From Tisala

And so men found gods in the sun, in fire,
Or in thunder, woods, or streams, in mountains,
Or in the household shrines of many lands;
And subject-matter gods – of love and war,
Fertility and grain – and built societies
Of messengers and angels round them.
Egyptians, Greeks and Romans thought it best
To keep the gods divided.

The desert-moulded Jews, finding their way
To monotheistic absolutes centralised
Their power in one omnipotent God.
And Christ and Paul and Constantine
And then Mohammed thus unleashed
A fearsome force for good and ill upon the world.
Not just the world of men, but through their mastery
Of much that lies between the quiet poles,
And in pursuit of their own righteousness,
They trample on the wonders of the earth,
Destroying lives and miracles of nature
They do not count or recognise.

The Story of the Stars and Gods

What did men think when down ten thousand years
They watched the sun sink in the sea
And saw the arching stars emerge,
Filling the darkening sky?

The guardians of the temples told them
'This is not for man to fathom out,
This is the wonder of the gods, beyond
The realms of men – just worship, and be thankful'.

But, talking in their little groups in the cool of night,
Did they not say 'As the sun sinks there
And will tomorrow rise behind us, it must travel
Overnight beneath us: it is going round';
And think perhaps that roundness is the key?
Some doubtless argued, 'You cannot pass beneath
The solid earth', and gave the gods their role.

The Greeks, taking up old sky-map schemes
Passed down from Babylon and Sumer,
Drew their constellations in the stars
And thus imposed that mythic view
Upon the starred night sky;
And long postponed reality –
The planets bearing still the names
Of Graeco-Roman gods.

But thinking Greeks – among them Aristarchus,
Who measured shadow angles all along
The shore of northern Africa – found
The world was round, and gauged its size;

So they could postulate: it is the earth
And planets that go around the sun.

But they were long eclipsed by Ptolemy's masterful
Grand image of a universe of sliding interworking shells
Above the earth, deemed centre of it all
And flat, immovably foundational;
And so diverted men a thousand years or more.

Until Copernicus, learning from the Greeks and observation
Produced his Revolution of the Heavenly Spheres –
The planets, earth among them,
Seen again to move around the sun;
Our place within the heavens changed for ever.

And from that place the planets and the sun itself
In time were shown to be just our locality
Within a spiralled billion-star-strewn disc – our galaxy –
So vast our world became the tiniest speck of dust.

But then, by new ingenious light-year scales, the galaxy
Was measured, and found to be a mere locality itself,
Within a universe so old and vast
It nearly lay beyond the power of comprehension.

Until, with instruments and means before undreamed of –
Radio waves and radio telescopes, and space craft
Orbiting the earth with cameras peering at the stars,
And probes sent out beyond the confines of our solar system –
Our questing minds pushed back
The history and the vastness of the universe;
Where, for the moment we stand unresolved,
At the edge of thinking power.

Now many say, trying to understand,
That gods – all the supernatural gods –
Are man-envisaged gods of our attempts
To bring some order to a little-comprehended universe.
And all will go, pushed out beyond the bounds of credibility,
Only surviving in sheltered, closed locations,
In certain lands however wide, and within the
Faith-filled minds where they're still needed,
And may – who knows? – be needed long into the future.

But otherwise are going, like the earlier gods of Egypt,
And many another earlier set of gods, their unreality exposed
By the brighter light of knowledge
Shining into the micro world around us,
And to the far recesses of the universe;
Leaving, beyond the edge of time and space,
The possibility of some great universal spirit
Uncovered or tapped into by our growing consciousness.

But balanced by the thought that spirit is a form
Of consciousness developed and developing
Solely within ourselves, as we slowly rose through nature
For many, many thousand years, rising
To be now where we are, and what we are.

Yet this is certain: for all our inter-stellar voyaging,
Our thought, our speculation –
For us, and all the living things on earth we know,
The centre of our universe and life is here,
Alive and growing on our precious
Only life raft home, the Earth;
Which, whether or not men think that there are gods,
Will need our love and wisdom to survive.

And if we humans fail, it may be that the world we know,
Our stellar knowledge, and the light of our intelligence
Will be snuffed out and lost, and the earth become again
A jungle and a desert for millions more of brutal, striving years:
Six million years of higher evolution wasted and destroyed
By just three hundred years of foolishness.

The Butterfly and the Spider

I came across a butterfly
Caught in a trap of spider's silk
Upon a thistle-top,
Flapping its wings towards exhaustion.

So, carefully, I broke the web
And gently disentangled it,
Removing the final clinging
Strands of shrouding silk.

It sat then on my hand, opened
Its wings, opened and closed three times,
As of to verify its freedom,
Before it fluttered, dancing, off.

And watching it I thought:
Death and survival
Are about control of power
By higher powers

With wider vision,
And so, in theory, more benign.
But did I send a starving spider
And her young to death?

If there is no higher
Intervening power than us on Earth,
In all great evolution's tree,
Then god–like power

And all responsibility
Are lodged in us.
By virtue of our higher consciousness,
We are perforce entrusted with the World.

On Hearing the News from Yugoslavia

We think there are no earthquakes here,
But – high among the branches of my apple tree,
Head and shoulders out above the crown
In the blue sky and warm October sun,
The red-flecked Bramleys on the southern side,
And nothing worse than earwigs and their dirt
Among the apple stems – my picking hands
Become for them a Bosnian upheaval.
Do they survive the fall of twenty feet?
And then for what – starvation first then death
In the orchard's cold-night autumn grass?

What now for those in that disintegrating country,
The winter tilt of earth spilling the cold
Of icy space among their mountain valleys?
And all around the canker seeping
Through the Serbian and Croatian towns,
Where power opposed by fear grows hate,
The fire of hate more strong than fear,
And leads to bodies of their people in the snow.

An earwig and an apple fall to earth.
The earwigs do not kill each other,
Their apple world is wrecked by outside force;
But in the Balkans neighbour now kills neighbour.
Where is a new philosophy, the healing vision,
So peace can drop again
Among the apple trees of Bosnia?

China Recalled

I hear the echoes of China from a thousand years ago,
And, further back, another fifteen hundred years,
In words and poems, paintings, paper works
And fibrous early records, back to the dimmer
Worlds of myth and archaeology.
Across these times there come the images of China.
Wooden houses set among wooded hills,
Village homes along the vast slow river valleys.
Gardens tending the calm of peaceful living,
Crimson peonies, the cassia trees, the yellow flowers
And pods of purging power, and phoenixes and peacocks,
With window views of mountains far away.
The Emperor's men travelling the ordered land,
And emperors' yellow silk in palaces,
The homes of bronzes – dragons, camels –
Guarding gateways, arches, doors.
Within, jade ornaments and artefacts,
The rustle of silk, slim waists
And wafting perfumes in the billowing curtained rooms.
The moon and stars reflected in the water
Of marble pools in gardens of delight,
The call of cranes across the peaceful land.

But too the grief of emperors on the death
Of concubines, the favoured chambers empty,
No longer perfume sweet, the alien dust no longer swept
And little piles of leaves gathered in the doorways,
And heaped in the corners of the courtyards.
While, beyond, seeking to hold the state together,
The Emperor's men, travel the troubled restless land

Before times turn, the western empire lost,
Though sometimes loss is gain and gain is loss:
The ambition of an emperor can undo a people.
And down the centuries disorder, insurrection,
Grief, and floods, and many lives and harvests lost.
Sages, tired of robes of office, exiled
To the mountains of the south, jagged above
The sea of cloud, seeking restful peace and shady woods,
Quiet living among the summer flame of flowers,
Beside the rice fields, and land tilled by the water buffalos.
While underneath, a yearning and lament
For the old harmonious order
Until new times and emperors arise;
The world awaits, needing wise emperors.

In a Chinese Home

The fish-tank in this house
Is lit to show the brilliant tropic fish,
But showing too the constant flow
Of bubbling water, assurance
That the flow of life and wealth enough to live
Will dwell within this home.

And through the doorway lies the quiet room
Of family remembrance,
Where anxious girls and youths may come
To think their thoughts to now dead grandfathers
And grandmas, and hear from them their thoughts
In silence, to guide or comfort them.

Children of India

Children of India
Emerging from sun-faded,
Dirt-streaked painted doorways,
Among the half constructed
Crumbling brickwork,
With tin roofs perched
On makeshift corner posts,
Awnings propped on wonky
Wooden uprights – emerging
Into dusty motorbike-filled streets,
Dust laden trees above,
Dust hanging in the air,
Dusty feet, dust everywhere;
Except their clothes, their
Smiles, their greetings:
Where beauty opens like a lotus flower
And shining hope unfurls.

Children of India II

I have seen the children of India,
In towns, on roadsides and deep in country villages,
The little ones bare-footed, dusty toed,
In scruffy clothes,
Holding still smaller infants;
The older girls, and women, in lovely-coloured saris,
Shyly smiling, going about their work –
Sweeping with brushwood, or with bundled firewood
Balanced on their heads, or fruit, or earthen pots.
The boys and young men in their western clothes
Already in the world of much-shared motorbikes
And working in the small town markets –
Fruit and veg piled high in roadside stalls;
The works of artisans – clay pots, assorted metal work –
Their livelihoods – spread out on the dusty ground,
Discarded boxes, plastic waste and plastic
Water bottles lying all around.
And I have seen their smiles and greetings
Returned them, smiling, shaken grubby hands,
Lined up for photos – families, groups of kids,
Coy teenage girls, enquiring students,
Young men and old – with arms round shoulders
For the photographs and memories of India;
And, well… in short, have loved them.

The Two Gifts

I gave my friend a stone,
A pebble from a beach,
But smooth and coloured thus:
One half, divided down a wavy line,
Bright yellow-brown.
But in the light half
Lay a patch of darker colour,
And in the dark half lay
A patch of lighter tone.

He looked at it
And held it in his hand,
Those slender pianist's fingers
Feeling round the edges of my gift.
Then I saw those dark eyes smile
And search me out.
'So – a yin and yan stone –
Thank you. I like it very much'.
'I found it on a pebble beach
Looking up at me –
And thought it should be yours.'

And when I went into his room
One time, the stone lay
On his desk among the books and
Papers of his much-enquiring mind.
Together we have climbed
High in the mountain ranges
Of life's philosophies.
I gave the stone,
He gave me happiness.

On the Unexpected Death of a Japanese Friend

Unexpectedly a star from the east
Fell out of the sky,
Plummeted to earth
And went out,
Leaving us dismayed and silent.
We all must follow her,
But she was the first of us
And the youngest
And should have shone longer
Lighting our sky,
Now diminished without her.

At the Ballet

She dances out the story of her love,
A tale of beauty, the movement of young life,
The harp-plucked music lifting all her hopes
And seeming unaware of us – watching
In silence in another world beyond the magic arch.

But darker music swirls up from the pit,
And chill and shadows fall across the stage.
Arms across her breast in self defence
Timorously she backs away in tip-toe tiny steps;

So vulnerable, unfolding innocence and beauty.
But still the darker music swells and evil looms
And tragedy begins.

The Master Class
a student pianist plays Liszt

In the fine new auditorium, the master class:
Centre stage, the huge black concert grand,
The famous pianist seated front row, centre,
And scattered round behind in tiered seats
The student's classmates, themselves aspiring
Instrumentalists, a few outside supporters,
And three teaching staff,
Whose work will also now be tested.

A slightly built Malaysian boy, sixteen perhaps
Or seventeen, comes forward, shining light grey suit,
A serious face, topped by half-cropped spiky Chinese hair.
He sits, adjusts the seat, is silent.
Then the hands move forward to the keys,
His head bows down as if to reach
The sound within and bring it from the depths.
And he begins – two low notes first,
Then the development, conjuring
By the magic of his memory-guided fingers –
No score, all held within his mind –
Cascading waterfalls, the wonderflow of music,
And Liszt's sonata re-created here.

And after, a scatter of applause and one brief bow
Before the lessons of the master class.
The concert pianist is not loose with praise,
The score now opened and spread out,
She picks and points, the phrasing worked at,
The magic disassembled in technique and nuance.
He starts, is stopped. 'Again'. 'No, more like this I think' –

She demonstrates. 'Again.' So on it goes, intensely,
But always aiming for enhancement,
The quest to master, and for soul-fulfilling art.

After in the foyer, I said, 'Well done,
I thought you played it beautifully - with heart and feeling.
Encouraging or daunting – was she a little hard?'
'Thank you. Oh, no! Encouraging! –
I think that she was right.'
The hunger there to learn, to be the best.
And many hours and months of work before him;
But the dream a little closer.

The Quiet Flow

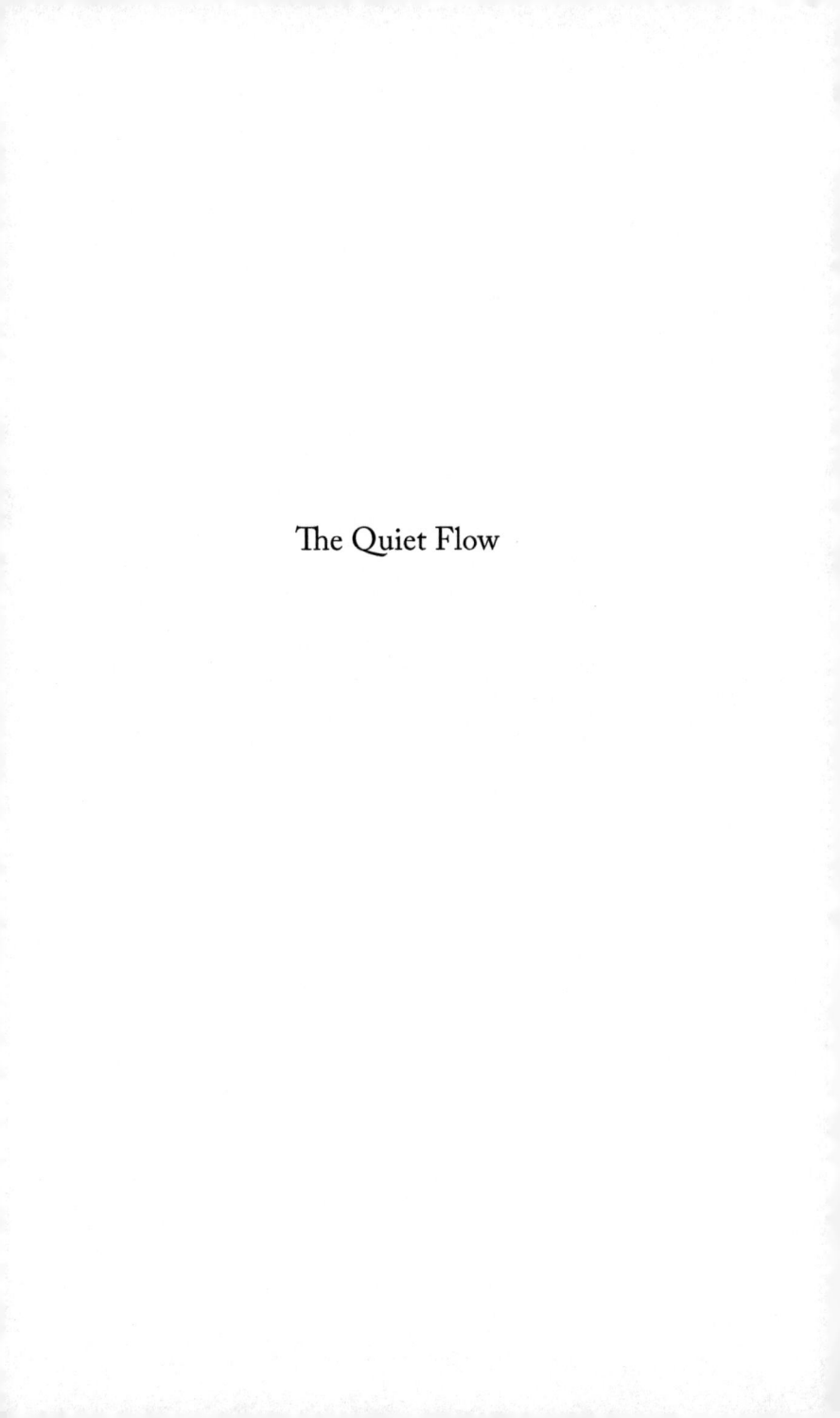

Tess

So she is gone; from us, from life
And this frequented garden.
No more our animated bundle
Of white fur will trawl the garden scents
Or look at us with keen enquiring eyes.
She lies as if asleep upon the grass
But for her open eyes, now sightless.
The tall dark cedar shades her from
The hot March sun under a blue sky.

The vet has now departed.
Quiet sad reassuring words were said
When Tess's life was closed and laid aside.
No more the puzzled painful suffering,
An end to all her brave attempts
To stand or walk, dragging her functionless
Back legs that could not then respond,
As if already part of her had died,
Sinking towards the earth.

And down the garden where she looked just now,
The daffodils and bank of primroses
And dappled grass under the apple trees
Beyond the white and purple-tinged
Magnolia still look on,
And all around the songs and urge of spring rise up.
No breath of wind, but then magnolia petals fall,
Trickling down between the twigs and branches,
Falling like tears to the moist ground.

And when we've dug her grave
Among the primroses and violets,
And the coming bluebell buds,
We line it with those same magnolia petals.
We wrap her in an old white cotton pillowcase
And lay her in the earth.
We say our words and all our sad farewells,
And tears and final petals drop,
Forget-me-nots are placed, and then
The soil, by handfuls as we kneel.

And all is done as best may be for Tess;
And for us too, by this drawn closer
To our own mortality.

Age

When we are old and incapable of love,
When your smooth beauty's like the rippled sand,
When slinky clothes no longer fit like gloves,
When minds no longer fully understand
And my good soldier fails to raise his flag
And health declines and tired bodies drag,
When prostates fail and hernias yawn
And aches and cramps bring sleepless dawns;
Then, in remembrance of our sunny days,
When we were lithe and beautiful in spring
And found long nights too short for lovers' ways
To satisfy the yearning young years bring,
We'll hold each other still in love's embrace
And ceaseless time a further while outface.

I Hope When I am Dead

I hope, when I am dead,
And the molecules that
Made me are dispersed,
That you will live and love,
And be much loved,
As in my little time
I've so loved you.

But in a little space –
Some unknown years –
When you too will release
The molecules of you,
Then atoms from us both will bond
So that, in time, we shall be joined again,
Each with the other;

And, wider, both of us with those
We loved who went before us,
Or those we will have loved
And who may follow after.
So thus our loves will have continuance.
Meanwhile I place this marker, dearest soul,
Of the love I bear you.

The Golden Coin
at Plum Village Buddhist Community, Martineau, France

In the deep countryside of France
The hamlet lies, where the plum trees grow
Among the gentle hills, neat fields, the quiet woods,
Among long grasses scattered with pink orchids.

There beneath the whispering aspens' shimmer,
The cherries shining red among green leaves,
Catching the dappled evening sunlight,
The deep bell sounds into the pagoda-guarded sky;

And the day-end call to peace is sung
By sisters clad in simple brown or grey,
Who know the calm of ancient wisdom
And send it out into the quiet twilight.

And after, simple food in silence, and lotus hands in thanks.
Give me the honour of washing down your plate
For that may wash away your shadows and your tears:
Compassion brought from war-torn Vietnam.

So to our old stone farmhouse down the road –
Briefly home to us who gather from the world:
Green tea, quiet talk, silence, breathing the air
Of gentleness: impermanent, like all, but giving life –

To find outside our door a golden coin, bearing
The Chinese wish that life may prosper and bring happiness –
Small parting token of a bigger gift: of friendship given.
But what I found there was the golden coin of love.

Windle

So Windle's dead: I read it
In the college magazine.
I never knew him, never saw him;
Knew just two things of him.
One: as vicar, married
My father and my mother
In the early months of war.
Two: each year that I remember
Through the letterbox there came
A plain white card of Christmas greeting –
Always the first card, ushering in
The modest plenitude of Christmas in our house;
Each year, for nearly forty years.
Until this year:
No card fell on the mat. 'Where's Windle's card?'
Somewhere a connection broken, despite
'We've never seen him since our wedding day,
But every year we send our cards.'

No answering signal from the void of years
Till now. But here it is, in 'Deaths':
'The Reverend H.A.J., war memorial
Exhibitioner, 1926 – 29'.
So, three: he was a fellow student with my father.
How many cards I wonder went each year
Through people's letterboxes,
And who said 'Windle's card has come'?
I suppose he thought them somehow his –
Marriages pronounced by him and in his charge –
And built a little network of his care
Against indifferent time.
And so I would record it.

Miss Adams

And when the old girl dies
There will be stripped
From that small room
A world of pictures and momentos,
Cared-for items, flowering wallpaper.
And a quiet past
Of gentleness will vanish.

The Photographs Not Taken

Under the plane trees
Among the market stalls,
A café in the leafy-dappled Aix
In summer, the hot sun
Splashing colours, wafting smells.
Such a beautiful girl:
She turned her head and entered mine.

On the beach at Antibes: red bikini
Lithe brown body, the girl who smiled at me;
But afterwards a slow lament
Because the memory of her will fade
In the decay of time, un-photographed,
That might have been preserved.

So here I put it down
Against the closing in of time,
That others may remember then
In their imaginations
Some once-seen lovely girl or youth,
Loved in an instant.
I think it may enlarge the souls of passing humans.

Autumn Leaves

The leaves are streaming once again
Down from the copper beech,
Golden, twisting, flying, soaring –
At one with the scudding sky.

How soon the year has passed me by,
Four seasons come and gone,
And still I struggle at my desk
To find the words I seek to share,

Before one day the copper beech
Again streams out its leaves,
Across the sky, across the grass,
But I not there to see it.

When My Body Dies

I know that I am dying by degrees,
So find each day the world becomes
More beautiful and precious,
Each part of nature – waving grassland
Or new fallen leaf, the flight of birds or clouds –
All things of wonder among the teeming miracles
Of colour shape and movement:
The symphony of Earth.

And so I still see smiles
Of younger men and women,
Their dancing eyes and lithe unblemished bodies,
As beauty unsurpassed,
The more revered and wondered at
Because I see the contrast with my ageing frame,
Which bears the scars and wear of many years.

But I have learned to see my body kindly
And recognise my silent life's companion,
My faithful, largely uncomplaining friend,
My partner and the other part of me
Who holds my life for me unsung
Sustaining and repairing patiently
The fabric of my being;
And thus allowing me to live.

For when my body dies
I think then so do I.
My mind and such soul as I have
Are bounded by this only guardian angel

That I know, and when he goes,
Or she, for x and y are both in me,
By sudden accident or failure,
Or long worn-out decay,
Then I go too and leave this precious world.

Now therefore should I care for this long faithfulness,
For though now weaker, still my working body
Permits my turning outward to the world,
To be of it a little longer yet
And love its art and music, gardens, trees,
Its skies and hills – so much of beauty;
And love as well the beauty in humanity:
An ageing, loyal, steadfast wife, the glorious young –
Family and friends spreading down the years –
And find new friendship and new love –
A hand on arm, a touching cheek,
An arm around a shoulder or a waist,
A hug or kiss, and happy eyes,
Smiling and talking with the ones I love.
Thus by degrees as time flows on,
I move in age towards my end, ready to say,
Goodbye, dear beautiful and striving world;
I loved you well.

Life and Giving Way

My viewpoint on the world will soon be shut
My window to all images through travelling time,
Past, present, future too will cease,
My brain's miraculous electric chemistry closed down.

How I have loved the privilege of life –
I do not want to leave the scene, but must,
And all the wonders of the waking earth
And those I loved and friends, the birds and animals,
Music, painting, cities, food, familiar smells,
Words and books, flowers, trees, the sky, the sea
And – on and on unceasing list of wonders.

And every one of these my senses
And the wonderbox within my skull provides.
But when my time is done, I'll happily
Give way my place, and wish for you to use it well.

More Fun on the Riverbank

The Seasons' Compromise

The tilting earth, reclining from the sun,
Brings winter from the deep cold universe.
The snow and ice creep southward as earth tips,
Our days reduce, our sunlight's weak and pale;
We should have been a thousand miles due south.

And yet, the tilt reversing, our cold world
Slowly warms once more,
And gives us greater wonder in renewal,
Bringing that blaze of light and life, our Spring.

But yet again: if summer's cool and wet,
I think, perhaps five hundred miles due south.

Freddie

Freddie is a little boy
Who loves to play with trains,
He dreams of steam trains every day
To exercise his brains.

He lays out curving tracks
With points, all on the carpet floor,
And sidings, stations, bridges next –
The scene grows more and more

Until the railway world's complete
With Mallard, Flying Scotsman too –
They leave the shed and circle round,
Past hills and hedges, past the zoo.

And over all this railway world
The mastermind is Freddie,
Until the day is nearly done
And his mum calls 'Supper's ready'.

Travel, Gin and Wine in India

A long and bumpy lorry-dust-cloud road
(Unfinished bridges, massive monsoon drains,
But little trace of tarmac yet).
When asked, our driver says 'Improvements.'
'When will it be finished?'
He stretches out an arm to indicate
The future smooth expanse of road,
'When it is ready.'

And after forty miles, a metalled road, the town.
We turn in at the swanky new hotel,
The gateman handsomely attired and turbaned,
Moustaches twirled – and, peace –
The ceaseless traffic fades away,
The trees umbrella us in welcome.
Inside the air is cool;
Reception, where the rooms are allocated,
'The boy will take your cases' (they have disappeared
Somewhere aboard a great brass trolley).
Our liveried escort shows us to our room,
And how the air con works, or should.
Cases appear – 'the boy' is grey-haired, fifty years or more.
A few rupees change hands, are graciously accepted –
'Namaste'; as is the service, 'Namaste' –
They teach you quickly here.
Kick off the shoes – the floor cool marble – wash,
Lie on the bed. 'We're meeting in the lobby.'

The lobby's vast, palatial, great high ceilings,
Dazzling chandeliers to match;

Modern frescos on the walls
Show brightly coloured scenes of gods,
And scattered round beneath, enormous sofas.
Where we meet. Our complainer's off the mark:
'There is no gin. No whisky either.'
The mirage fades.
'I've had words with the manager.'
She wants to show she'll not be put upon,
The one who likes to sort out trouble,
And can often find it.
The waiter comes. 'The wine list, please' she says
'Yes certainly. Yes, red or white?'
'No, no, the wine list, *please*.'
The waiter - little English – stumped.
And anxiously he tries again, 'But red or white?'
'Oh God!' Defeat. And silence.
A second voice, the gravel voice of our excessive smoker
Beside me says 'I'm sure the red is excellent –
A large one, please.' She smiles at him.
A burden lifted from the waiter's face.
The sun comes out.
'I bring it very soon at once.'
A hand goes up: 'Two white ones, please –
Yes large,' indicating bucket sized.
The sunshine spreads. 'Most definitely.'
The gravel voice asides to me
'I don't care if it poisons me. The silly witch.'
And then you know you've got a travelling companion,
And the laughter can begin.

On Reading Too Many Poems for a Poetry Competition

Not bloody Ithaca again –
And all the reverenced isles and myths –
Poor Icarus, endlessly plunging to his death, again,
And nothing to be done to stop it,
Or Vince van G – that bloody ear, again.
Why do they hold them so? – yes, yes I know –
Good stories to be kept alive, renewed –
But why as if they were the limits of the poets' world?

Mind you, far better these than
Blackest, black-hole grief, again,
Obscure in word and misery,
Or clichéd Gothic weird,
Or formless shifting paradigms, again,
Or simply strange incomprehensibilities.
Though sometimes, searching in among them all,
Glimmers of something, maybe, maybe good
If only they could be understood.

But at the end,
The little pile that's left:
And there they are, the ones
Which keep us searching, hoping:
The gleams of gold.

The Ballad of Tom Drinker

"Would you ever be after drawing a drink?"
Thomas asked the barman again.
"That I would," says he with a knowing wink
Across at his red-faced wife.
So the beer mugs clinked, and the liquor flowed
(And God only knows how much Tom owed),
For Tom was a drinker born and bred
Always lonely and drunk when he went to bed.
But poor old Tom drank his inside out,
And they laid him down with a bottle of stout,
And an epitaph over his head which read:

> In Memory of Thomas who loved drink so dear
> That the cause of his going to heaven was beer.

Pop Lyric

I met a girl
Who turned her head
And then she looked
At me and said:

'Where've you been?
I've been looking for you
And all across my life I knew
I'd know you when I met you.'

We danced all night
Then she went away
And I was looking for her next day
And her face was haunting me

I sat by a river desolate
Till I felt an arm round me
And heard a whisper in my ear
"If you love me, I'll be always here.'

But something's keeping her from me
I've never seen her more,
Though I looked and asked around the town,
Left messages on doors.

So I love her still
And I'll search until
I find again that haunting face
Though the world's a wide, wide place.

The Ballad of Felix Cavalier
a ghost story for winter supper parties

Once I stayed in a grand old house
Of the Jacobean age.
That night I wandered through the rooms
Down endless corridors
Through doors that led me on and on
Until I reached a huge dark hall
Lit by a blazing fire.

And there in the flickering light there sat,
In an oak-carved chair by the fire,
An old cavalier dressed in midnight blue,
And on his lap was curled up a cat
Who raised his head and looked at me
With bright green eyes
While his black-tipped tail
Began to swish to and fro.

When the Cavalier saw me he smiled and rose,
Putting the cat on the floor,
And he came towards me
His arms outstretched
As if I were a long-lost friend
And we had somehow to make amends.
And the strange thing was as he came to me
I knew what I had to do.

So I stood my ground and opened my arms
And as we hugged there was something there –
Not flesh and blood, but more than air,
And he looked at me with a grateful eye

And I thought and knew he now could die.
But it's hard to hold ethereal things
And his smile and his face both faded away
And his arms collapsed
And his chest caved in,
And as he sank down
I sank down with him
Till all that was left was a pile of clothes –
A doublet and breeches and dark blue hose.

Then I awoke in my moonlit bed
And thought how that dream had entered my head.
But the strangest thing of all was that
I thought I heard the purr of a cat
And I felt something weighty by my feet
And the something stirred and stood.

And there was a cat with a black-tipped tail,
With eyes of the brightest green.
He purred and purred as if to convey
A thank-you for something he wished to say.
Then he silently jumped from the bed to the floor
And though I looked swiftly I saw him no more.

Next day when I questioned my host about this
He laughed and pointed behind me and said
'This is the only cat that lives here.'
And I saw in the picture on the wall
A Cavalier seated in a large hall
Stroking the cat that sat on his lap,
With its black-tipped tail and bright green eyes
That looked at me with a calm surmise
And I swear the trace of a smile.

Notes

First and foremost poems should be able to stand on their own. But it can be helpful to readers to have a little more information about the poems, and particularly their contexts, than the poems themselves do or should give. For those who would like them, here are a few short notes.

The Opening Stream

The Student's Dilemma (P. 31)

University students in the early 1960s were a small minority – about 3% of British young. And there were only a few universities. MacMillan's premiership reflected the country's standing in the previous half-century, which despite Attlee's government, was still slightly Edwardian and empire-orientated, though the winds of change were well under way. In the humanities, university meant a broad education. Future employment, thought to be plentiful, was often rather hazily further down the road.

Salute to the Cinema (P. 32)

Written in Dublin, in the early 1960s. Dublin with its share of poor, but fascinating, cheap and a delight for student living, where the cinemas (tickets nine old pence), theatres and pubs were all socially important. At Trinity College, students were sent to the Henry Street Market, where it was said the spoken language nearest to Shakespeare's still survived. In the theatres it seemed that half of English literature had been written by the Irish. Ireland, poor but rich, and on the verge of economic revival under Sean Lemass, and later by joining the European Economic Community. But at that time the Hollywood dream dominated the cinema.

Town Bands in Germany (P. 33)

Written after hitch-hiking in 1960 – only fifteen years after the death of Hitler, and the destruction and division of Germany; but the economic rehabilitation had begun and the first bricks of the European Union had been put in place. Confidence was beginning to return to the people. In those days, students hitch-hiked all over. I'd come down through France to Italy – as far as Rome, and was hitching back. My first time in Germany. Quite different from the black and white newsreels of the war – colour and lovely old towns and houses.

Weather and Authority (P. 34)

Four episodes of European history from the Spanish Armada to Hitler's Germany and Russia. The pride and arrogance of kings, emperors and dictators undone by simple miscalculations; but at terrible and increasing cost.

Springtime in a Coppice (P. 36)

Weather as a poetic topic is perennial: the clampdown and consequences of winter, as in 'Weather and Authority' (p. 34), followed by the renewal of life in spring. This little poem reflects the seemingly unchanging pattern of the seasons, familiar in the northern hemisphere since before time immemorial. But now less so for many millions because of the spread and disconnect of city dwelling, with its built up environment and further merging of the seasons by central heating and air conditioning. And, on a bigger and more ominous scale, because of advancing climate change. 'The

Seasons' Compromise' (p. 113) may take on a different slant. Future weather poems may be very different.

The Cuban Crisis (p. 37)

But was there to be a future? In the cold war years Russia (as we commonly called the USSR,) was seen as one of the world's two great superpowers. The USSR and the USA – communist and democratic – ranged against each other in almost religious ideologies – each deeply suspicious of the other's ambitions and intentions. Each held several thousand nuclear weapons in an arms race to stay ahead. And always there was the horrible fear of the button being pushed, either by miscalculation, or as a pre-emptive strike out of weakness. The threat hung over everyone on a daily basis – lives, families, careers, the future, in a way very difficult to imagine today. Into this danger sailed the Cuban crisis in October 1962. The poem was my student reaction, written in Dublin in the middle of the critical days, when we waited helplessly, with the world's future in the balance.

A Student's Turmoil (p. 38)

For those who went to University there were many options and job opportunities. The dilemma here was to chose, often with rudimentary guidance and much ignorance about both the job and oneself, which to pursue, at a time when love and hormones were also a source of life-shaking turmoil.

Forebears and Descendants (p. 40)

As with weather and the future, different too is the way we look at ourselves in the light (where known) of modern biological knowledge, and expanded consciousness of how we come about, with its consequences for our view and conduct of our lives. So too our relationship with nature and our fellow animal life, as in 'A Seabird's Life and Death' (p. 42) and 'The Butterfly and the Spider' (p. 83).

We Were Gods (P. 41)

A group of students of wide disciplines on an expedition, walking and talking on the mountains of Rhum, a beautiful almost uninhabited Scottish island. On fire with new knowledge, questioning philosophies, religion, ambitions, idealism. But already grappling with other realities – careers, the wonder and misery of love – reflected in some of the poems that follow.

Shakespeare's England (P. 51)

A poem about an England, as we were taught it, that was leaving behind the Medieval and Catholic mind, embracing the Renaissance, Protestant Christianity and commercial expansion, edging towards democracy and becoming an age opening out into new and wider worlds. A process that was part of the European worldwide expansion, for good and ill, in the sixteenth and following centuries. But the imposition of empire, the coming of science, and the development of the modern world lay in the unknown future.

The Broader River

In Persia, 1974 (P. 55)

That year I went to Iran, Persia we still tended to call it, at a time of momentous change. I went as part of an advance party of a geological and geographical expedition planned for the following year. This involved meeting various levels of officialdom, including senior ministers in the Shah's government. Iran was run by the Shah. They had celebrated, in 1971, the 2,500th Anniversary of the founding of the Persian monarchy, taken as the reign of Cyrus the Great (560 to 530 BCE), which had ushered in the great days of the Persian Empire, then the most extensive empire at that time ever to have existed in the world – from Greece in the west to India in the East. They had celebrated in a memorably lavish feast and ceremonials at Persepolis, the magnificent ruined capital of ancient Persia. The events were attended by most of the world's reigning monarchs, and many presidents and prime ministers. The Shah presented himself as a reforming monarch, as his father Reza Khan had before him, in trying to secure the country's place in the modern world. But the power of both was autocratic, and anything that threatened it was dealt with ruthlessly, though ostensibly within the legal system.

That the whole edifice of the Shah's regime would be overthrown within five years, though perhaps foreshadowed, was not known when I was there in 1974. The poem was written after some time in Tehran, a visit over the Elbruz mountains to the Caspian shore, and a few days in the beauty of Isfahan. The poem was largely written, or at least jotted down, on the bus from Isfahan. We went to Shiraz, the city of nightingales, roses and poets, and to the spectacular ruins of Persepolis, which lay to the south. Further east, on the plain, was Pasargadae.

Thank You Letter to the Poets (p. 58)

First is Chaucer, who established the character of English poetry in his writing, led by *The Canterbury Tales*. And who introduced the iambic pentameter into English poetry, with momentous effect. Imagine Shakespeare, Milton and Wordsworth without that line, which so suits the rhythm of the English language. Then Shakespeare: incomparable. No more need be said, except the importance of renewing his work enjoyably and intelligibly to each new generation. And then Coleridge and Wordsworth, evolutionary in verse form and language, and in the subject areas of their poetry, with their view of nature and the sublime. Such debts we owe our poets.

The Trials of Poetry (P. 59)

And then, in the twentieth century, there was Eliot. Certainly he caught the bleakness at the end of the First World War, and produced a language to express it. But we were continually told how subtle and sophisticated *The Wasteland* and afterwards the *Four Quartets* were, without, for many, ever understanding why, or being convinced. There was something deeply unsatisfactory about these poems being presented as the great poems of the twentieth century. If they were, something was wrong, like the unquestioning assertions of biblical truth we were taught when young; reservations began to take root.

These grew over the years, so that *The Wasteland* and the *Four Quartets* became for me a blockage on the wider truths about the existence of human kind. This poem resulted. It was written about twenty years ago.

In The City, Seminars (P. 63)

I worked for a period as a City solicitor, and found much to enjoy in the commercial buzz. I was working, in a junior role, with musicians both classical and pop, and on the contractual work that lay behind concert performances and record deals; and the legal side of feature films required for those to reach cinema screens. But I never really made a City solicitor, as 'All Those Grey Solicitors' (p. 65) may indicate. Much later on I returned to general commercial law, with elements of film and journalistic work, and their accompanying financial side. For Eliot, banking and the City were viewed as a form of living death, though he earned his living there for a period. This poem, written in the 1990s, I hope reflects different aspects of the City and worldwide commercial skills.

Fortieth Birthday (P. 66), AND *New Year's Eve Party* (P. 67)

Two poems on two aspects of time and how we view and use it. Benjamin Franklin, said 'Do not squander time, for that's the stuff life is made of'. It is a theme returned to, in 'Age' (p. 101) and two or three of the poems in the third part of this River's course.

The Princess (P. 68)

Princess Diana's life was cut short by her death in 1997. Her whole brilliance on our scene seemed like something of a fairy story, but as in them, bad things happen, and sometimes they are very sad. This little poem was therefore written in the mode of a fairy tale.

Since By My Age (P. 69)

A small but pivotal poem for me. I retired from the law in 1998 to write a philosophical novel. The narrative is centred on the appalling history of twentieth-century whaling. Tisala, a Blue whale, seeks human contact to understand and appeal against the genocidal slaughter. He meets David, a young biologist, learns to speak (like the Houyhnhnm horse in *Gulliver's Travels*) and brings an enquiring mind to bear on human affairs. The ideas side of it is an enquiry into the state of humanity and how we got to where we are in the early twenty-first century. For some reason, though published, *Tisala* (Blue Mark Books, 2015) has not yet become a best seller. Perhaps Tisala got it right when he questioned whether: 'Great novels arise in the minds of authors rather more frequently than they are put on paper'. But as authors will, I still harbour a hope for it, and find encouragement by remembering a critique of *Moby Dick* when published, which scornfully dismissed it out of hand. Alongside that large endeavour poetry continued, which meant digging out the poems and drafts scattered through my life as well as writing new poems attempting to extend the range.

Two Universes (P. 70)

The first of a small group of following poems on aspects of science and scientific discovery, and their effect on us, as in 'Four Fires' (p. 71), and 'Time' (p. 73).

Sleep (P. 74)

In 2015 I heard a biologist lecture on sleep at Exeter College, Oxford. Biological research apparently shows that sleep, a form of sleep, enabling animal life to sustain and renew itself, is ubiquitous on earth. It has been part of animal life from the beginning, and is found in primitive forms going back three billion years. Without sleep they say there would have been no development of life as we know it, including, of course, us.

Heavenly Physics (P. 75)

Physics, the basis of our fundamental understanding of the physical universe, is stuck between two apparently irreconcilable theories, Newtonian and quantum. This is good ground for poets. They can succinctly show hypotheses and discoveries to a wider public than might understand the maths and terms of a technical and scientific presentation. This poem may strike some as having absurd ideas, but some physicists are working on them; and that is how revolutionary theories and advances often start out. All depends on proof. But a successful unification of all physics could transform our view of reality in many areas of life.

On the Nature of Luck (P. 76)

And so to philosophy and religion, and science and morality, aspects of which arise here, and in 'From Tisala' (p. 78), 'Victoria's Vespers' (p. 77), and 'The Story of the Stars and Gods' (p. 79).

Victoria's Vespers (P. 77)

Do the arts broaden our humanity, as well as entertain? Here, in new music for a then new age. I remember reading once that Verdi never heard a Beethoven symphony. Beethoven somehow, out of those sounds, conjures a sense of nobility, of moral strength and courage. As for us, we are lucky to have at hand through technology the whole range of western 'classical' music, increasingly spread around the globe by the skill and dedication of new generations of young musicians from many countries, as in the 'The Master Class' (p. 94). And that is only a part of the story. All the world's music is available to all through technology and travel, the sense of harmony from China, spirituality from India, and many different facets of humanity from many lands. Understanding and pleasure go hand in hand, and can draw us together.

From Tisala (P. 78)

The double-edged legacy of some of the world's great religions is well known. By divine revelation and authority or by tradition, they promoted their own versions of theology and morality; but, historically, often enforced them by intolerant violence, which in some quarters sadly still continues. This poem engages with the theme. As Tisala observed, 'religions are creations that will take much unravelling', and he questioned whether 'the religions of men have been an interim attempt to impose order and meaning on a then little understood universe'. But in any case it has become clear that, in both the secular and religious world, a moral code acceptable to all is badly needed, perhaps along the lines he proposed, based 'on what wisdom we have acquired'.

The Story of the Stars and Gods (P. 79)

A similar theme on the role of history and religion also appears in this narrative poem, raising questions both on knowledge and religion, and beyond to climate change.

The Butterfly and the Spider (P. 83)

Taking a human-centred view of the purpose of creation, some of the formal religions have not done very well in preserving our planet. Can an understanding of biological truth and our place in nature do better? The question becomes increasingly urgent, by reason of our enormous and increasing numbers and planetary exploitation, and the resultant increased task of education.

On Hearing the News from Yugoslavia (P. 85)

In the twentieth century, ethics and morality, from whatever sources, both religious and secular, have often failed in the face of political, ideological and tribal-racist pressures. Here, in the collapse in the Bosnian War (1992 – 1995) after the falling apart of Yugoslavia.

China Recalled (P. 86)

The poem reflects China as an old civilisation, going back to Confucius (about 550 - 480 BCE) , and on through the centuries of political ups and downs, upheavals, and golden periods, such as the late T'ang, (about 730 – 860), a time famous for its poetry. A number of images in the poem may be recognised from that. Old China lies behind modern China in its history and role as a leading nation in the world.

In a Chinese home (P. 88)

And two thousand years later parts of the Chinese heritage not only survive, but are practised and have social value. The poem describes the present scene in the house of a friend's grandmother.

Children of India I AND *II* (P. 89 AND P. 90)

India, another old civilisation, a breath-taking and beautiful country, also with many daunting problems. How one hopes for India and China, albeit in their different ways, to prosper, and develop into good and peaceful friends of each other and the world. Wise leaders are indeed needed; as they are elsewhere.

The Quiet Flow

Tess (P. 99)

Our much-loved family dog – a white West Highland Terrier. Intelligent, bright-eyed, an avid chaser of squirrels, and watcher of animal programmes on television.

Age (P. 101)

A time sonnet, linking with 'Fortieth Birthday' (p. 66), harking back and forward.

I Hope When I am Dead (P. 102)

A Nirvana-like concept, but arrived at through the route of chemistry and biology, though familiar from Buddhist thought.

The Two Gifts (P. 91), AND
On the Death of a Japanese Friend (P. 92)

Two poems on friendship, which tends to get under-sung in poetry, though valued highly in full lives. Yin and Yan, sometimes represented in the west as opposites – light and dark, good and evil. But in the Chinese, and Taoist understanding and tradition it is really about the contrasting essential unity of all things in life – light and dark, evil and good, male and female, active and passive.

The Golden Coin (P. 103)

Plum Village is a community of Buddhist nuns founded by Thich Nhat Hanh, a Vietnamese monk and thinker, after he was exiled from Vietnam having tried to broker a peace in the Vietnam War. A place deep in the countryside east of Bordeaux where peace and friendship may be found.

The Photographs Not Taken (P. 106)

Opportunities going and coming, and incidents of happiness observed, in the south of France.

Autumn Leaves (P. 107), *When My Body Dies* (P. 108), AND *Life and Giving Way* (P. 110)

Towards an end: but with a deep gratefulness for life.

More Fun on the Riverbank

The Seasons' Compromise (P. 113)

Environmentalists tend to be earnest, with good and increasingly urgent reason. This was written in easier less aware times, when holiday travel abroad was becoming the norm for many. But maybe there is still a place for a bit of humour: sometimes it can raise a question or awareness. Perhaps also it marks what we may be losing.

Freddie (P. 114)

Poems for children, suited to their world and enjoyment, are a way of giving them a lifetime subscription to one of the better aspects of humanity. This, with a bow to Robert Louis Stevenson, was written for a grandson, who, like many young boys was enthralled by steam trains, *Thomas the Tank Engine* and all that world of boyhood imagination.

Travel, Gin and Wine in India (P. 115)

To anyone who has not been to India: go. And so far as you can as a traveller rather than tourist, though the one facilitates the other. Scenes of dust and poverty, yes; but wonders await you – colour, smells, chaos, delight, and many smiles.

On Reading Too Many Poems for a Poetry Competition (P. 117)

For some years I've been involved with one such literary festival competition. That people turn to writing poetry is encouraging; and there are increasing numbers in the Young Poets age range (16 to 22).

It is a medium that responds well to crystallising and recording important experiences in people's lives, and there is much to be welcomed. But, as argued in the Preface, poetry is a craft, like many others, that is difficult to master.

No doubt some of the poems in this book will be criticised. But I hope that others will give pleasure. Very broadly speaking about 80% of poems submitted to competitions are probably in a range between not good and downright bad; but mostly the authors are not told so.

A few years ago I wrote a note on failures of craft that often spoiled writers' efforts at poetry. Such judgement is always subjective. But it was not allowed, on the basis that it might discourage too many entries, and lead to a fall in fee income, and consequent prize reduction. But I still think people who write poetry want to write better poetry, and quite a few might find it encouraging rather than discouraging. So I hope the present poem will be forgiven.

The Ballad of Tom Drinker (P. 118)

Dublin days, 1960s. Humour, but also compassion, in which the Irish excel. A very small affectionate offering. A stagehand's footstool to the great Irish tradition: Goldsmith, Farquar, Sheridan, O'Casey.

Pop Lyric (P. 119)

If I were better at it, I'd try to set this to music in a ballad or folk style. Maybe someone will. It needs a beautiful lilting tune.

The Ballad of Felix Cavalier (P. 120)

We were invited to a boxing day supper party. Our hosts' daughter, who was organising the entertainments, said everyone was to bring a poem or ghost story. So I wrote this as a contribution. Humour helps the world go onward.

Acknowledgements

These poems might not have been completed but for the help of many people over the last six years, starting with my family support and encouragement, and particularly Toby's invaluable help with the manuscript.

Simon gave me the space and time to work in Oxford, as did the Bodleian Library. I have received kindness and help from a number of busy academics at Oxford colleges, and from friends – too many over the years to list – but including Chris, Tony, Lucy, Christopher, Theo, Emma, Terry and Samuel.

To all, named and unnamed, and to all who caused me to write, I am ever grateful.